How To Develop An Attitude For Success

Jim Shafe
&
A.G. Strickland

CAREER TRAINING CONCEPTS, INC.
ATLANTA, GEORGIA

Copyright 1988 by

James C. Shafe
&
A.G. Strickland

1st Printing ....Aug 1988
2nd Printing ....Sept 1988
3rd Printing................June 1989
4th Printing ....October 1989
5th Printing ....July 1990
6th Printing...........January 1991
7th Printing................June 1991
8th Printing ....October 1991

Published by:
Career Training Concepts, Inc.
2191 Northlake Parkway • Suite 160
Atlanta, Georgia 30084
(800) 367-3523
(404) 723-1345 (GA)

Printed in the United States of America

Library of Congress Catalog Number: 89-91805

ISBN 1-877846-00-7

ABOUT THE AUTHORS

Jim Shafe and A. G. Strickland established Sales & Management Training of Atlanta, Inc. in 1973. They specialize in creating training alternatives that are customized to fit any organization...seminars, video, audio, train-the-trainer, packaged programs, etc. Together Jim and A. G. represent over 55 years of firsthand training experience in all 50 states. They have:

- Formed Career Training Concepts, Inc. in 1987 to address a broader range of career needs. Almost 200,000 students benefited from this training during its first year of operation.
- Listened to over 300,000 talks concerning personal experiences related to attitudes and success.
- Helped thousands of individuals gain confidence in themselves in front of groups and in their personal lives.
- Increased productivity in sales representatives and managers throughout the country in all types of industries.
- Assisted the military in recruiting and retaining soldiers for a strong national defense.
- Researched, designed and conducted programs to meet the specific needs of such clients as the Coca-Cola company, The Equitable, Orkin Exterminating, Rollins, Inc., Potash Corp. of Saskatchewan, Zep Chemicals, National Vendors, Lockheed of Georgia, Universal Art, Majestic Portrait Studios, Life of Georgia, Canal Bank, Blue Cross/Blue Shield, University of Tennessee-Chattanooga, Canadian Industrial Chemicals, Ltd., U. S. Army National Guard, U. S. Coast Guard, U. S. Navy, U. S. Army Reserve, ROTC, Heery Program Management, Inc., SunHealth, Georgia State University, Kem Manufacturing, Warren/Sherer, Amax Minerals, Snapper, and others.

Other books authored and created by them include:

Career Direction
Goals for Success
Front Line Leadership
How to Sell Successfully
How to Get Action: Key to Successful Management
Total Quality Leadership

INTRODUCTION

How to Develop an Attitude for Success?

Learn the secret. It's easy. It's close at hand. You probably already have it and don't know it. You'll find it is the common thread in the fabric of all successful people. You'll begin to discover it early in the first chapters and it will start to glow as you move along. You'll end up using it.

This book will help you develop a greater insight into yourself...the starting point for any real improvement. Your efforts in this material will be directed toward self-understanding, personal motivation, goals and leadership.

The lessons in "How To Develop an Attitude for Success" should prove to be an invaluable part of your professional development.

Here's to your success!

Jim Shafe
A.G. Strickland

TABLE OF CONTENTS

1

KNOW YOURSELF

Psychology can be a scary science for many of us. Most people figure it is somewhat over their heads. This science covers everything from private therapy to industrial testing and word association to a simple chat with a trusted friend. Neurologists, counselors, experimentalists, behaviorists, and religious philosophers all practice psychology to some degree.

Psychology is a wide field that is a rapidly growing area of concern. It is performing a huge chore in educational testing and counseling, communications, and human services. It is growing in importance and application daily.

PSYCHOLOGY CAN
BENEFIT EVERYONE

To really benefit from modern psychology, you usually have to be rich enough to afford psychotherapy, or personally troubled enough to seek professional assistance. In the past, if someone went to a psychiatrist or "shrink," many people labeled him or her as "crazy." You probably remember a Presidential election when a Senator who was running for Vice-President ended up withdrawing from the race. Why? He was embarrassed when it was revealed that he had seen a psychiatrist. Fortunately, we now understand and virtually everyone recognizes the value of being able to tell someone his troubles. When this someone can listen objectively and not condemn us, a great deal of personal stress is relieved.

The high cost of psychiatric counseling, or therapy, makes it difficult for those who are sometimes quietly desperate to get the relief which professional psychology offers. A much deeper satisfaction, peace of mind, a sense of well being and abundant energy are available for all of us. Psychology is one area of human knowledge which can open up these possibilities.

Out of the thousands of experiments, theories, and hypotheses which are found within the field of psychology, perceptive and concerned people have distilled many valuable concepts. Let's look at these, but put them in a form that is easy to understand and use.

SELF-IMAGE
PSYCHOLOGY

The study of psychology indicates that the complex and multifaceted concept you have of yourself controls all your reactions, all your desires, ambitions, hopes, plans, and feelings.

What you think of yourself and how you respond to your self-concept or self-image has a great deal to do with your happiness and success. If your self-confidence, respect, esteem, reliance, assurance, and acceptance are weak, it is because of your low self-image.

We can use a simple diagram (see the diagram below) to illustrate how your self-image affects you. All your thoughts, ideas and emotions must be consistent. Ideas that don't fit in are rejected. If you think you can't do mathematics, no one can tell you to become an engineer. If your self-concept does not include getting along with people, you could hardly be talked into becoming a salesman. The center of this system of consistent ideas is the "ego-ideal" or self-image, the base from which all else is built.

Ideas which are not compatible or consistent with the system are rejected, "not believed" and not acted upon. Ideas which seem to be consistent with the system are accepted or "believed." After all, how often have you heard someone say, "Well, that just isn't like me."?

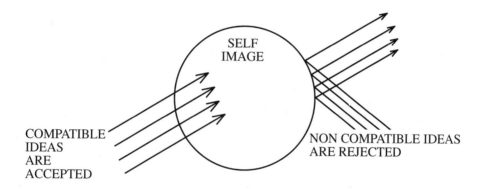

In other words, if you see yourself as a dud, then any ideas or comments that reinforce your opinion of yourself as a dud are accepted. Any comments that portray you as a super sharp individual would be rejected or at least cause you to be suspicious.

Here is an example to illustrate our point. Roger's father had wanted to be a teacher, but he failed to complete his education. To make up for his deficiency, he raised his son with the idea that he should become a teacher. From his earliest years, Roger began to think of himself as a noted teacher, author and lecturer. He behaved like school was his private property. Often other children were bothered by his attitude. The principal of the school, however, sided with Roger and defended him publicly. Since Roger considered school important, play was just "kid stuff." Roger ignored any attraction to sports and games and spent time helping the teachers. He graduated from grade school with top marks, but the children already called him "The Professor."

In high school, Roger studied hard, got good grades, dated no one, and began toying with the idea of becoming a researcher in languages. However, he also discovered girls and began to notice that people shied away from him. The girls couldn't take him seriously, so Roger swallowed his pride and studied harder.

In college, Roger's social inability and frustrated romantic needs became painfully obvious to him. He visited the chaplain and got insight into the reason for his backwardness. Roger began studying less and tried to become more socially active. However, the image of the professor lingered on as a basic moral obligation and he felt guilty for not studying.

It is easy to see how Roger's self-concept controlled all his behavior. It determined what he would like to do. Notice how certain things were accepted as being consistent while other ideas were rejected as not appropriate?

YOUR
COMFORT ZONE

Let's take a look at this self-image thing from a slightly different angle. All of the experiences you've had are mentally logged away and cause you to see yourself as "comfortable" performing certain activities. We could say that these activities are within your **"comfort zone,"** while other activities, ones you've never tried or tried unsuccessfully, are outside your comfort zone. Let's call the area outside your comfort zone the **"uncomfort zone."** In diagram form, it would look like this:

Uncomfort

Comfort

ME

Zone

Zone

So far, so good. The bad part is this — psychologists and neurologists tell us that only a small percentage of our brainpower is actually utilized — no more than 10 percent. That means that **90 percent of our capabilities are squandered or wasted in the land of "I can't do that."** Worse yet, as we get older, we are inclined to feel uncomfortable trying more and more things, and we attempt fewer "new" experiences. That darn comfort zone starts to become increasingly restrictive and limiting, just like hardening of the arteries. One will eventually kill you, and the other will squeeze all of the courage out of you. Hiding in your comfort zone will turn you into a person who says, "We always did it this way" or "That's not like me." Now, think about it for a minute. Don't you really hate it when people resist change by saying that and are just plain scared to try anything new?

Personal growth comes from stretching — not resting in your comfort zone. **You can spend the rest of your life hiding in your own comfort zone, or you can fight it. When you hear yourself say, "That's not like me", a mental light should click on that says, "Psst, hey dummy, let's try it — don't stagnate!"** Attempting different and new activities, mentally or physically, academic or athletic, will cause you to grow and develop confidence.

A BIG PITFALL

It is almost impossible to have positive thoughts about external situations as long as you hold a negative concept of self. You must first have a positive idea of who you are and what you are worth. If you think you are a failure, no amount of "positive thinking" will help. You must first change your opinion of yourself. To illustrate, let's look at a young man named Tom. Tom swore that he was going to be the top salesman in his company. He acted cheerful, spoke firmly, and knocked on lots of doors. However, he found himself getting tired, nervous, easily upset, and dreading sales situations. He forced himself to go through with it anyway. He became so tired and depressed that he started to sleep late in the morning and quit early in the afternoon. What Tom remained unaware of was his own true self-concept.

As a boy, Tom's parents broke up and his busy and tired mother gave him little affection. Tom felt left out and started hanging out with some rough people his own age to compensate for his lack of companionship and family life. He got into trouble, and the judge gave him a choice of jail or enlisting in the service.

Subconsciously, Tom felt that he was an unlikable and worthless person. When he tried to act differently, it took a lot of energy to keep up the front. Using too much emotional energy gradually dragged Tom down to weariness and depression. This carried on into his adult life and his job.

Fortunately, he told his sales manager about his feelings, and his manager explained how he had gradually forgiven himself for his own youthful indiscretions. Tom finally began to realize self-acceptance and recognize his hostility toward himself.

The two men laughed over themselves, and the sales manager made Tom look at his good qualities. Soon Tom changed his basic self-concept to a more realistic and updated version. He no longer repressed the bad thoughts about himself from the past, but he brought them out in the light where he could deal with them and accept them.

Notice...all the positive thinking in the world didn't help Tom until he quit believing that he was a worthless and unlikable person. Only then was he able to accept himself the way he was. This acceptance includes being able to laugh at himself.

Take another case: Julie made a vow to be a well-known educator, prominent in her field. That goal became all important to her and, consequently, all consuming. To grasp the significance of this accomplishment, you must examine Julie's past. She was the eighth of nine children in her family. Her father had drifted in and out of the home during all her childhood years. The family never quite seemed to stabilize, and the lack of education seemed to be holding him back. Her driving ambition was education. Not only was she the first in her family to ever finish high school, but she went all the way through and received her Ph.D.

After receiving her Ph.D., she immediately started trying to "move" in the social circles she felt were appropriate for a "Doctor" and tried to project the image she felt she should have. But it was phony. That makes the BIG difference. Acting out this role took an incredible amount of energy, and other aspects of her life began to crumble. Her marriage fell apart and her career assumed a much higher degree of importance than even her children. The problem seemed to be that Julie subconsciously felt unlikable, unattractive and unworthy. She put up a facade. No amount of "acting" out the image she thought she ought to have made her accept herself the way she was, with all of her flaws. Only if she had done this could she have developed a happy, healthy life and successful relationship with her family. Sure, she could have strived for the Doctor's image, but only after she quit fooling herself.

If your hopes and dreams clash with your idea of yourself, forcing the issue will not help. If you basically feel you are unworthy or unlikable, no one can convince you that success is possible. You may be able to fake it or "rev" yourself up for awhile, but eventually it will catch up with you. Start with accepting and liking yourself as you are. Then you can begin to fulfill your hopes and dreams.

UNDERSTANDING
YOUR SELF-IMAGE

Dramatic evidence of the power of self-image psychology has been shown by Dr. Maxwell Maltz with a number of American and European prisoners. Certain prisoners who had very ugly, "criminal" faces with huge noses, bad teeth, hooded eyes, jug ears, etc. had plastic surgery performed on their faces. Within twenty-one days there was a sudden rise in self-esteem and self-confidence on the part of most of the prisoners. People who had been grumpy and hostile became open-minded and congenial. Men who had refused to talk to anyone began to open up and do things for others. People who openly hated and rebelled started listening with interest and conviction.

The peculiar thing, however, was the fact that while most of the them responded that way, some did not. So obviously, surgery wasn't the complete answer! Something else contributed to the change.

Careful psychiatric evaluation pointed out that what had really happened was a tremendous change in the prisoners' ideas of themselves. Whereas they had always considered themselves ugly, obviously vicious people, a new face allowed them to toy with the idea that perhaps they were decent people after all. Once this idea became excitingly real, then all behavior started to change. Change increased hope. Hope caused enthusiasm. Enthusiasm caused good relations with others. Good relations convinced them that they were decent individuals, etc.

Thus, **your self-image is the key to your personality and your human behavior.** It defines what you can and cannot do. It also defines what sort of personality you wear.

If, like the prisoners, you begin to see yourself differently, then you will behave and act differently. Your actions and behavior will reinforce your self-concept, and you are then on the way to developing a much improved self-image.

But you must remember that a change in self-estimation and self-concept must go along with a change in your behavior and action. Unless your actions change and your behavior changes, your new self-concept will fail to materialize. You cannot just think your way into a new self-confidence; action must follow thought.

BUILDING
A SELF-IMAGE

Your self-image has been formed gradually and unconsciously by your experiences since the day you were born. This creates such an indelible impression on you that mere words and thoughts are simply not strong enough to counteract the weight of a lifetime of experience. Only new impressions and new and fresh experiences can build a new self-image. You will never "discover yourself" by reflection, but only by watching yourself in action!

What do we mean your self-image was built unconsciously by experience? Your personality reflects the sort of person you think you are. Interestingly, the person **you** think you are never precisely matches the person **others** think you are or the person you **really** are.

It goes like this:

- **Who you think you are**
- **Who you really are**
- **Who others think you are**

In your mind, you carry around a ton of "excess baggage" from all the embarrassing, bad or negative things that have ever happened to you. When you had to sit on the bench in Little League or were screamed at by your coach, you may have seen yourself as not as good as the other players. After a handful of these experiences, it is easy to begin to believe it. When you didn't get the special birthday gift you wanted from your parents, you may have felt hurt and perhaps unloved. When you were embarrassed in front of your class, you probably made up your mind you'd never talk in front of a group again as long as you lived. (We've worked with thousands who carried scars from poor handling in classroom speaking.) You may still tell yourself, "I just can't talk in front of a group." Sound familiar? If so, beware! Your "excess baggage" is crippling you mentally.

Unfortunately, we often let this negative excess baggage cause us to become negative to others. Instead of realizing the problem is within, we fight new ideas, new training, new implementation — or even the old. It's easy to take an inside battle of feelings out on others. **If a kid runs through the room and falls over a stool, he gets up and kicks the stool, not himself. It's easy for us to revert to childhood and take it out on outside sources instead of considering, "Could it be me?".**

If you have had an overdose of negative impressions, then you

may have become "negatively oriented." This negative attitude reinforces your feelings of inadequacy to such an extent that it is difficult to accept and believe positive statements about yourself. People
who constantly react negatively to life often reflect a troubled personality. On the other hand, a healthy personality allows you to react
with confidence and a positive attitude to your environment. Let's
face it, most of us could stand to improve our outlook and enjoy our
lives a little more.

A NEW YOU

So how do we go about it? Consider this: **Clinical testing has
shown that our nervous system cannot tell the difference between a real event and a vividly imagined one.** Having trouble
believing this? Then try a personal experiment. Answer honestly.
Have you ever suddenly sat bolt upright in bed, instantly awake,
sweating profusely, because your dream had just scared the day-
lights out of you? Now, try to tell yourself that your "system," your
subconscious, your adrenal glands, and your sweat glands knew it
was "just a dream." If, in your imagination, you see yourself being
humiliated, you'll feel the picture very vividly indeed and will probably end up taking action that will, in fact, cause you to be humiliated.
If you can visualize yourself being calm, relaxed and interested in
someone, then you'll be able to act that way with that particular person.
If you develop your ability to vividly imagine yourself a certain way,
then you can become that person. This, of course, starts with an
understanding of self as a sound beginning.

The fact that the nervous system cannot tell the difference between real or vividly imagined experiences allows you to create
wholesome experiences for yourself; to feel them, to hear them, and
to live them. You can begin to see yourself in a different light. **You can
actually visualize yourself in a pleasant experience and then take
action to make it happen.** This changes your behavior and reinforces the new self-concept. For example, basketball coaches have
experimented with having their players visualize themselves making

shots, etc. Later, they actually shot better.

So, even though your experiences and reactions have caused you to form an idea of yourself, **you can change that idea and positively alter your own self-image.**

2

YOU WERE BORN TO SUCCEED

YOUR SUCCESS
MECHANISM

A study of basic biology gives us a lesson about success. All living things have a built-in guidance system or success mechanism to allow them to grow, develop and overcome obstacles — to accomplish their goals. This guidance system works automatically. A plant automatically pushes its roots down and its leaves up, and thereby achieves success and fulfillment as a plant. A squirrel instinctively collects nuts at a certain time in the late summer. The automatic guidance system tells the squirrel his next project or goal. Even if he has never experienced a winter before, he has only to react to natural instinct.

But a plant, a rosebush for example, doesn't have a choice about what it's going to do. It can't suddenly decide to produce tomatoes instead. Nor can the squirrel suddenly determine that he'd rather save AT&T stock instead of hazel nuts. Their goals are set for them

23

and they succeed naturally.

One has only to look at a few National Geographic specials on television to become totally awestruck with this incredible guidance system that everything in nature, including us, has built in to it.

One of the most remarkable creatures is the salmon. Salmon have incredibly delicate sensing mechanisms. A salmon can detect one drop of ammonia in over a million gallons of water. When they are born, they completely absorb their surroundings — temperatures, smells, swiftness of the current, kinds of rocks, silt, chemical tastes and so on. Only one stream in the world runs, feels, tastes and smells exactly that way. This ability to photographically imprint surroundings is called "eidetic memory".

At a particular point in the salmon's development, something triggers a response within them. They gravitate toward the ocean absorbing their impressions of the stream as they go along. At a point of maturation in the ocean, a new signal triggers their return home for protection. The old programming activates and the salmon are able to return to their original spawning grounds. The salmon, as remarkable as they are, cannot intentionally change their fate. Nor can other parts of nature. Only man can change his.

Man was not only created, but he is also a creator. We have the same kind of guidance system as a plant or animal, but the system will function only for survival unless we set a goal for something else beyond mere survival. All other forms of nature have their goals more or less "pre-programmed". You and I do not. You and I must decide upon our own goals. In another publication of ours, <u>Career Direction</u>, high school students are asked to take a test to see which vocations seem to interest them most. In fact, aptitude testing, interest testing, and value testing constitute a whole industry. This is evidence of the incredible range of occupational choices or goals we may project for ourselves.

Unfortunately, this need for man to actually make a decision and set a goal is why there are so many people who feel their lives are meaningless. The vast majority of them have never set a goal and they just wander aimlessly through life doing whatever seems to come next. After a while they can't even dream of themselves as successful, and all hope is lost.

Man has the same success mechanism to succeed as a human being, that a rosebush has to succeed as a plant. We are obviously made to think, to act, to carry out, to perform and to create. We are programmed by the Creator to succeed. We can easily determine from a study of elementary science that each of us has the automatic creative guidance system composed of a brain and nervous system, and that it works like any other servomechanism, guidance mechanism, or computer. The system is a machine which you, the human operator, can program to work for you or against you.

To grossly oversimplify the complexity of your mind's functions, let's say your success mechanism performs two major activities: (1) It stores and gives you answers when you need them, and (2) it keeps you on target. As an analogy, let's consider a standard naval torpedo. A torpedo has a guidance system which is aimed toward a clearly visible target. The guidance system zeros in on the target and, as water turbulence changes the course of the missile, negative feedback from the guidance system corrects the error and directs the torpedo to its target.

BUILDING A SELF-IMAGE

To build a positive self-image effectively, you must keep a clear and definite goal in mind. You must also allow your automatic system to correct your mistakes and react properly to your positive and negative feedback. Too often, when we hear "negative" feedback, we are inclined to blame ourselves for doing "wrong." Think back to the example of the torpedo. It had done no "wrong." The water turbulence simply caused it to get off course and the negative feedback made its guidance mechanism aware of the need for adjustment. **You and I need feedback, both positive and negative, to make us aware of needed behavior adjustments.**

Some of our goals are never completely realized because we do not think in terms of end results. It is amazing how keeping your sights set on the objective will allow you to conquer obstacles along the way.

Sometimes individuals forget to focus on the goal and end up magnifying minor flaws along the way. The end result can become clouded by what seems to be some absolutely insurmountable obstacle. Often, when put in perspective, they are relatively minor points. This is why it is necessary for you to keep your eyes on your goal and maintain your enthusiasm.

There are some principles of human behavior which we can relate to the missile with the automatic guidance system. Regardless of the errors or outside influences, the guidance system automatically corrects your course. The most important point is not to stop — but keep making constant progress forward. Here are several rules that can help guide your efforts:

1. Don't Be Afraid To Make Mistakes -

Fear of making mistakes will cause you to attempt only those things which you know you can do perfectly. Now really, how many things can you do "perfectly?" In many offices or work environments, the boss, in an effort to improve performance, constantly corrects the mistakes of others and criticizes. If we aren't careful, we can easily find ourselves doing the same thing at home with our children. Constant criticism can quickly destroy confidence. It can make it almost impossible for you to sincerely believe you can set or even dream of accomplishing a meaningful goal.

2. Don't Give Up -

Determination and persistence are amazing qualities. They are like "after burners" or "booster rockets". When you depress your mental "determination button," your whole system will really focus 100 percent of your energy and concentration on your goal. It's like wearing blinders to all distractions and you simply refuse to give up.

You've probably read of examples of this **intense focus of energy and determination** in cases where a vehicle fell on someone and a father or mother was able to use "superhuman" strength to actually lift the vehicle off the victim. Some would say this is also an example of "blind faith". We can buy off on that description also.

3. Don't Over React To Negative Feedback -

Sometimes it is easy for us to allow negative feedback to totally demoralize us. Most people are well-meaning when they criticize us. They honestly believe they are helping us or doing it "for our own good". However, it is very easy to give negatives, and most people are accustomed to doing it. They don't find the same joy in giving positives. **Don't let the negatives bend you out of shape.**

If we receive their feedback properly, it can help and sometimes we can make appropriate adjustments in our behavior. If, on the other hand, we choose to get defensive or start feeling self-pity, the feedback will be harmful.

Also, there are times when we simply don't perceive the feedback to have the same meaning as was intended. For example, when Jim was four years old, his older sister started calling him "Big Ears," not a very glamorous nickname. Off and on, she called him "Big Ears" for about twenty-six years. He was so embarrassed about the size of his ears, he hated to get his hair cut short. Basic Training in the Army was anticipated with anxiety because he knew he'd have to wear his hair short and his "Dumbo" ears would stick out! Only when he was thirty years old did he discover that she really was harassing him for being a nosey little kid who overheard and then repeated everything! Hey, this he could handle. He knew that and it had never bothered him. This is really just one more example of the "excess baggage" that we haul around.

LEARNING TO USE
YOUR "COMPUTER"

Soon after the development of the computer, we became aware of the fact that our own minds function in somewhat the same way. As we all know, the computer has the ability to store information and allow the operator to "access" or retrieve this information easily. We said that your brain or your automatic creative success mechanism stores and gives you answers when you need them. That was one function of the mind that we outlined earlier.

If you are familiar with computers, you know that after being programmed, the computer operator simply feeds the problems or data into the machine and then **leaves it alone**! You also have a "computer" in your guidance system. It has been programmed by many years of experience. It has huge memory banks. When you buy a computer, you select a system which has finite storage capabilities. Generally speaking, the less memory capacity, the lower the cost. Your mental "computer," on the other hand, seems to have an infinite storage capability. In fact, our "human computer" is so impressive that current researchers at the California Institute of Technology, Georgia Tech, Carnegie-Mellon University, and others are designing "super computers" patterning "parallel" systems organized like the human brain. If you learn how to feed problems into this incredible personal "computer," leave it alone and trust it. It can give you almost any answer you need.

In 1960, a neurosurgeon was performing brain surgery on a twenty-six year old woman. The patient was required to remain conscious during one phase of the surgery. Accidentally, the doctor brushed the cortex of the brain with the back of his scalpel. Immediately some astounding things happened. The woman relived a childhood experience that she had long before completely "forgotten." **She didn't remember the experience — she relived it.** She could actually see her grandmother, hear her talking, taste the cake, and smell the warm summer afternoon!

Everything we have ever done is, in fact, recorded in the system. At this stage of human development, we know little about retrieving stored data. We do know that relaxation, enthusiasm and other positive feelings make information more readily available.

In some of our classes, we conduct a relaxation exercise in which, after getting very relaxed mentally and physically, the participants are asked to visualize the home they lived in as a ten year old. They are talked through various rooms in the home and asked to "look around and see what you notice." Invariably, people see many objects they had long since "forgotten." The exercise continues to include people they see, sounds they hear, and even smells they detect. People often "relive" childhood experiences that had been locked away or bottled up for years.

Repeat: Everything you have ever experienced is stored away in your brain — just waiting for you to push the right recall code button.

Humans, similar to the salmon, simply absorb their surroundings, thus programming themselves for success. At each moment, information of every sort is being taken in and stored. We experience a rich and interesting life, if we are completely open to it. Most of us, however, shut out full experience by shunning a great deal of the life around us.

Carol and Mary were twins, unlike each other emotionally. Carol was small and lively. Mary was larger and shy. Both had always earned good grades, but Carol had decided to enjoy everything she did. Her sister had not. One afternoon the girls attended an industrial tour through a machine shop of a large manufacturer. Mary felt out of place and rather scared. Throughout the tour she was very conscious of her clean knit dress and put a lot of effort into being careful, avoiding getting dirty or getting hurt.

Carol, on the other hand, put aside her fears and became fascinated by the roar, smells, and sights of the factory. A few weeks later when both girls were interviewed by the same company, Carol remembered peoples' names, she could explain the manufacturing process, and she was able to relive much of her initial experience. Her sister only experienced fear and did poorly on the job interview.

Carol was open, sensitive and aware, and absorbed a great deal of information into her "computer." When asked questions, her information was close at hand. Her sister was conscious only of herself and protected herself against the environment. One was programmed for success. The other, because of her intense focus on self, was programmed for failure.

From this example we can see that worry, fear, anxiety, and pressure can cause our system to function poorly. Making yourself focus on what is going on, instead of how scared you are or how you feel about what is going on, will cause the system to function much more effectively. We need to learn to live warmly and creatively, instead of with tension and fear. If we live cheerfully, ideas will flow more freely. These ideas can help you establish clear cut goals. Let your guidance system take over. If you draw on the vast amount of positive information about yourself and your life, you can bring many impressions together into a clear, vivid and believable picture. Once you can see yourself as successful, your guidance system will help you accomplish the fulfillment of that picture.

For this reason we strongly urge "creative visualization," "autosuggestion" or a "quiet room technique." These ideas of creative visualization are probably not new to you. They suggest that you set aside time daily to recall your periods of happiness, past successes, good experiences, and recent accomplishments so that you will see yourself as a more valuable person. Once you see yourself in this light, it becomes easy to see yourself accomplishing your goals. The ideas and feelings will be received so clearly and vividly that action has to follow. **With thought and actions, your dreams can materialize.**

3

DON'T SELL YOURSELF SHORT

ACCEPTING
YOURSELF

Once you accept the fact that your brain has stored away all your past experiences, knowledge and abilities, then you can readily see that "It is all in there — it is within me to succeed." In recognizing this, what you are actually doing is accepting yourself, accepting what you know, and accepting what you've done. It basically means that you believe in yourself, or that you have self-confidence. Such an act is caused by and induces self-knowledge and self-respect.

A prominent psychologist stated that, in his opinion, a very real purpose of psychology is to get people to understand themselves and then **accept themselves**. "This is the only real basis of any new changes, development or growth," he said. "People don't know how to look at themselves as a total individual. What I mean is that they fail to see all of the facts. Their attention becomes fixed on a few points about themselves and they fail to see that overall, they are good —

considering all the facts."

We can easily see this tendency in areas other than personality. For example, you may have a minor wreck and dent your automobile. The car may still run great, yet there is a tendency to let the whole automobile deteriorate as a result of one insignificant flaw. The flaw takes on unrealistic proportions and the importance of the proper function of the automobile is diminished. The same thing is true with ourselves. You and I have faults. We also have failures. It is easy to focus undue attention and importance on them and feel guilty and worthless as a result. **We allow our failures and mistakes to loom menacingly on our mental horizon as we try to take on new challenges.**

For example, most people feel they are terrible at remembering names. Why? Because they focus on the times they forgot someone's name and were embarrassed. Now the more they worry that they'll forget and be embarrassed, the more likely it is to happen. Instead, attention should be focused on the dozens of people you do remember and accept that, "Hey, I can remember names!" After all, even your own mother probably calls the names of every member of your family sometimes when she is trying to call you. Certainly she hasn't forgotten your name, it's just a brief "dumb attack" that makes it difficult to call your name. A guy in one of our classes called these "brain cramps."

You can have faults and failures, yet you are still important and worthwhile. No happiness or success is possible unless you are able, perhaps only little by little, to find out who you are and accept that person as he or she is.

The satisfying thing about self-acceptance and self-respect is that it means believing in the real you, just as you are. This mental attitude of acceptance is transferable to other "selves." This simply means that **if you can accept, like, and respect your true self, then you should be able to accept, like, and respect others**. If you can accept yourself as you are, then others become more acceptable also. Soon you find yourself liking and accepting more people. After awhile the old saying of Will Rogers takes on actual possibilities: "I never met a man I didn't like."

Recently in a hotel, Jim met a housekeeper named Jo who was exceptionally warm and friendly. It was at the end of a long, hard workday. The last thing he wanted to do was converse politely with this little lady. However, in her gentle, warm manner she told him all about her granddaughter who is coming to live with her next year when she starts college. As she talked, her pride and love radiated and he found himself very interested. Jo commented on all the nice people she meets through her job. He asked her, "Seriously now, have you ever met anyone, anywhere, who acted ugly to you?" She said she never had. The reason is obvious — as we said, **if you accept people, they will respond in kind.**

Sure you have faults, but you also have your good points. Take a moment and consider some of the strengths and weaknesses you feel you have when it comes to dealing with others. Five qualities I think I have that make people like me or want to deal with me are as follows:

1. _____
2. _____
3. _____
4. _____
5. _____

List three of your shortcomings that limit your ability to effectively handle or get along with others:

1. _____
2. _____
3. _____

The inclination we have to dwell on our shortcomings is one of our least desirable characteristics. Most of us simply do not accept ourselves for what we are. We think we should be different, better, smarter, richer, more attractive or more educated. We think the present self is just plain inferior.

This is a terrible personal injustice against yourself. It means that you are not measuring yourself against your own goodness, accomplishments, personality, norms, and standards. You are measuring against someone else's standards. Face facts. Of course, there are people who are smarter, richer, better looking, etc. So what? There are also people who have less money, less intelligence, and are a whole lot less attractive than you. **You can really only compare you to yourself, not to others.**

We have been taught by philosophers through the years that we should love and appreciate human nature. The most constant example of human nature around you is yourself. If you can love yourself, you can learn to love and respect others.

To illustrate the concept of self-acceptance, let's turn to an experience that happened to a man named Bud. Bud had always hated people who were braggarts, and he took enormous delight in criticizing the stories of others. On one cold and stormy night, coming back from a trip through the northern part of his sales territory, Bud watched in horror as a car in front of him slammed on his brakes to avoid a deer. The car started into a slide and then twisted off the highway, landing upside down in a raging creek. Bud and a long-haul truck driver were the first people on the scene. They stepped into the water and carefully lifted out the unconscious victims.

Bud described his reactions later. "As I approached the car, I was just praying that it wouldn't be too far out under the water. I think that if I had had to duck under the water and up into that black hulk, I wouldn't have had the guts to do it. I was excited and scared and was actually pleased to be in the first line of action.

"We got them all out and no one died, but I sure learned some things about myself and about human nature in general.

"I found out that I actually saw the wreck as an opportunity to prove my courage. I noticed that I stayed around much too long afterwards because I was hoping that the press would come and interview me or take pictures. I was actually hurt when my wife didn't pay too much attention to the whole story. What I learned was this: I'd like to have glory just like any other braggart. It's just that I'm too ashamed to try it. I learned that **people brag because they want to be appreciated.** From now on I know this. Despite my desire to want glory for it, I will act in emergencies. All braggarts, whether they are noisy ones, like some people I know, or quiet ones like me, are eager for attention."

Bud learned to accept his real self and soon found that he understood others better. If you can accept your self, your feelings, your background, your abilities and short-comings, then you can accept almost anyone. You can probably think about it and realize that most of the braggarts you know are praising themselves because that's the only way they get any recognition. You might be amazed how a simple compliment is appreciated by these people. When others give you appreciation, you don't need to heap it on yourself.

YOU MUST DECIDE
WHO YOU ARE

Since many of us were raised to believe that the standards of others are the "right" ones, most of us grow up feeling at least mildly inferior. If we use absolute values or the norms of others, we will always come out second rate. This was the case with Pete.

Pete had an older brother who was good at everything. Pete was an enthusiastic youngster who enjoyed competing with his older brother in everything. His brother didn't like it particularly, but tried to be a good sport about it. Pete loved to win but became sullen or despondent when he lost. If Pete's brother lettered in football, so would Pete. If his brother dated a pretty girl, Pete would try to date one prettier. Pete was often quarrelsome and touchy.

One day, Pete's brother announced that he was going to be married the following year. In keeping with his competitive attitude toward his brother, Pete eloped before six months had passed.

Pete now had to assume many responsibilities, and he quit college to look for a job. He was a tough competitive person in lots of ways, but he had difficulty staying in any one line of work.

Pete became disenchanted and the job changes caused financial worries. He and his wife began quarreling, so Pete went home to visit his folks for the weekend. He began to feel like a failure and his feelings of guilt were becoming stronger.

He spent a long time talking to his father and over the weekend he came to the realization that he had been a copycat all his life. If someone did something, he had to do it also. All his life he had basically been copying everyone else. He had never really done anything he wanted to do, and he didn't have the slightest idea of what he really wanted in life.

He realized that he felt inferior because he immediately looked to the sharpest person in any situation as being the one he had to beat. He could not accept his own immediate level of proficiency. It was now clear to him why he had always been such a poor loser. For the first time he began to look at his own abilities and goals and he quit comparing himself to others.

You must first learn how to compare yourself with your own norms or standards. This means you must be able to look at your background, your education, and your experiences to generally determine how these influences helped create the person you are today. **It is that person you have to understand and accept. It is that person you must decide is an okay person. It is that person you must decide you like.**

GREAT EXPECTATIONS

We hear so much about how things "should have been," or "what I should have done," It is easy to have 20-20 hindsight. When people compare themselves to absolute standards, they are often hurt. This is because they are trying to measure up to the other fellow.

When comparing yourself to all the "shoulds" and all the "musts" and all the "bests," you can come out as a rough specimen. This makes you feel inferior.

People with inferiority complexes then make a second horrible mistake — they try to "catch up." They try to do too much, too soon, too hard, too fast. They try to be the absolute best in some area or in all areas, constantly trying for perfection. In some cases, they even try to "out pitiful" other people. When someone mentions a problem, they've had one that was worse. When someone mentions an accident, they've had one that was more horrible. An illness? You guessed it. They've been sicker. They refuse to accept anything but the perfect self even if that means perfectly awful. They are on such a narrow road that they have no room for mistakes. To make a mistake eliminates perfection. So, when mistakes are naturally made, they are magnified out of proportion. Here is a simple example to illustrate the point:

Martha's parents were very judgmental. They felt they could judge the character of people by the clothes they wore and the way they handled themselves in a social setting. They drilled into Martha's brain that she should not associate with certain people because they were "bad." Any time she slipped up and exhibited any distasteful habits, she was criticized.

This attitude had a profound effect on Martha. It made her dread mistakes of any type and feel guilty when she made them. She became so picky and critical of others and so outspoken and bossy that people felt uncomfortable around her. This attitude often left her lonely and out of touch with her friends. The more critical she became, the fewer invitations to parties she received. Her friends even started working to avoid including her.

When Martha finally married, she tried to be the ideal mate and expected the same of her husband. On the one hand she tried to do everything with perfection. If she burned a meal or forgot a dental appointment, she became easily upset. On the other hand, many things her husband did were not acceptable either, since she judged him by the same norms that she judged herself. Due to her over-restraint, Martha became extremely anxious and would overreact at the slightest problem. Her outbursts made her feel guilty since the outburst was "bad" behavior. She then tried harder to repress her natural feelings and a vicious cycle of behavior was set in motion.

Accepting reality is the first step toward self-realization. Most of us look at ourselves "as we would like to be" instead of how we actually are. Getting to know the real self is interesting, even fascinating. Getting to know others is even more so. If Martha could have stopped striving for perfection, she may have found out that her real self was a very likable person.

So, to whose standards are you comparing yourself? How do you think others see you? Write a statement here describing how you believe others perceive you.

_____

_____

_____

MAKING SUCCESS
A REALITY

It is well to accept the idea that comparing yourself to others causes an unrealistic self-image. When comparing yourself to others, you run the risk of developing feelings of superiority or inferiority. **There are simply no inferior or superior human beings**. The equality of man is the only proper truth. In fact, only a person with an inferiority complex can even desire to be superior. Psychoanalytic research confirms that a superiority complex is usually a sad and hopeless coverup for feelings of inferiority. Consequently, trying to act superior tells others just how little confidence you really have.

Making an effort to quit being inferior only reinforces the idea that you are. That's why self-image psychology does not start with self-improvement. If you have to improve yourself, it means that the present self is unacceptable. People who consider themselves unacceptable cannot react properly to life, despite all kinds of will power. Remember the illustration in Chapter I on how your self-image functions? Self-image psychology tries to cause self-understanding first. Self-acceptance first — Self-respect first — Then with a positive ego-ideal, you believe and react to the good in life, rather than the evil and hopelessness.

To sum up, at first, you don't really change your personality at all. You look at yourself under a new and more realistic light. Only when you accept yourself, can you be yourself. New experiences build a new self-image, a new behavior and a new personality.

Whenever you experience feelings of inferiority, ask yourself these questions:

1. Why do I feel this way?
2. How did I get the habit of reacting this way?
3. Is what I feel really true?
4. Is it that important?
5. Can I do anything about it?
6. Can I accept it?

You begin to get sold on yourself by understanding your own human development, by dropping the standards of others and finding your own. You improve by remembering the things you've done well and by reflecting on previous successes so that you can see yourself in a favorable light. When we see ourselves favorably, we become more enthusiastic, a quality that shapes success.

Everything you need for success is already inside you. **By remembering your past success, you can assure yourself that some success is possible right now. You recognize, most importantly, that all things considered, you are a success right at this moment!**

4

FREE YOUR CREATIVITY

YOUR MIND
WILL WORK IF
YOU WILL LET IT

Sometimes we wonder how some people can say just the right thing, how they manage to slip in just the right comment to make everyone laugh, how they manage to "think-up that angle" or where they get that good idea. How do they **do** it? They seem so relaxed! Relaxed?

Would you believe that being relaxed is the cause of their creativity? **They aren't relaxed because they're creative. They're creative because they're relaxed!**

Most of us would like to be creative and so we think and think and think and try to come up with great ideas. Earlier we talked about the mind performing functions somewhat like a computer. A computer can only give back information or compute based on the programs and data that have been programmed into it. Once properly programmed, however, the computer operator can feed in data, ask questions, and simply leave the computer alone to do its thing.

We also said that the subconscious, our storehouse or our "computer" aspect of the mind, would function well if the temperature were correct. That is, if we are relaxed and if the time is right. For this reason, we need to act and live as if the answer already exists, because it really does already exist, buried somewhere in our subconscious. Trust your subconscious.

Instead, what do most of us do when trying to solve a problem? Well, first we try to avoid the suspicion that there is a problem at all. Then we reluctantly acknowledge the possibility that one could exist. Soon it starts nagging. We think about it on the interstate, during lunch, while jogging, during our favorite T.V. program and while getting ready for bed. The problem haunts us throughout our waking and conscious hours. We need an answer. It should start to become obvious that in this state of mind it is difficult to arrive at a meaningful solution.

Unfortunately, most of us were trained very early in life to solve our problems by thinking about them with conscious thought and effort. We sit down and concentrate on a complex math problem, history assignment, or business problem. This sort of process is like trying to build a highway with a toy bulldozer. It simply isn't big enough to do the job. Many times the conscious mind isn't either. The conscious mind can only handle one idea at a time. One of our biggest stumbling blocks is trying to use the forebrain far too much. The forebrain is no more equipped to handle the problem than a computer operator is equipped to do the computer's job.

Remember, you have all the memory banks you need. The job of this vast information storage and retrieval system is to digest and properly file large amounts of material and then issue the information upon request. Your mind will naturally do all of this if you will just let it! **So do your homework, study the problem, learn all you can about it, and then trust your subconscious.**

DON'T TRY TOO HARD

Earlier we discussed the "difficulty" of remembering names. How often have you tried to remember someone's name only to find that it came to you after you gave up and quit trying?

Most of us, thank goodness, have had a number of experiences like this, and they make us kind of wonder. The amazing thing is that we are surprised when the answer suddenly appears. We shouldn't be surprised at all. Our mind is made to function that way. The key is to give attention to the following:

1. Really look at the problem.
2. Think about it.
3. Then forget about the whole thing.
4. Go about what you were doing.
5. Allow your mind to kick in the answer automatically.
6. When it does, focus your energy and attention on that one thing and take **action**!

In his book, <u>Vital Reserves</u>, William James indicates that if we want our ideas or solutions to be varied and effective, we must learn to quit worrying so much about the outcome. He says to do all of your worrying and concern early on...while trying to decide on a plan of action. Once you decide on your plan and action is in order, leave the worrying behind and simply do your very best. Continuing to worry actually will restrict your performance. He says you should, "unclamp your intellectual and practical machinery and let it run free and the service it will do you will be twice as good."

You can probably think of examples when you struggled to solve a problem, trying virtually everything in your power, only to result in frustration. Perhaps, much to your surprise, however, you suddenly arrived at a very simple, workable solution. Maybe you even woke up in the middle of the night with your idea in mind. That's the ultimate in relaxing and letting your "machinery" run free.

Most of us worry about how we are going to pay bills, get a raise, change jobs, pursue a career, or improve our marriage. This act of worrying gets us so up tight that the very artery to an answer gets clogged. Rather than become increasingly expert at worry, anxiety and dread, we should trust our mental equipment and go through the following process to solve a problem:

FIVE GOOD
QUESTIONS

1. Is there really a problem?
2. What is it?
3. Do I sincerely want to solve it?
4. What is everything I know about this problem including the cause?
5. Is there a solution?

If there is no solution by the time you get to number five, and you have honestly studied all the facts you can — honestly, then the only thing you can do is to forget about it. Relax! Sleep on it. Refuse to dwell on it. Play golf. Read. Do anything! Just keep your conscious mind away from the problem.

If you continue to worry, you only jam the mechanism and nothing will happen. If you really do forget about it, the answer will usually come very quietly and simply later on. Once you get the answer, act on it. Don't get hung-up on your mistakes. Positive action is important because the "guidance system" has to be in a moving missile before it can correct anything.

One further thing should be said about ideas which are generated in this manner. Once the idea is received, it needs to be acted upon quickly. That doesn't mean, though, that you should not check out and refine the idea. Very often, the subconscious provides answers to the overall problem, but working out the details is a function of conscious thought.

If you want to be a creative person, you will have to learn to let your mind relax. **You cannot force it to become creative, only allow it to do so.**

Here are some guidelines for freeing up your creativity:

CREATIVITY
GUIDELINES

1. Learn all you can about the situation or problem.
2. Relax and learn to trust your subconscious.
3. Enjoy life around you. It will help you to relax and keep your mind receptive to ideas.
4. When the answer comes to you, take action.
5. Do one thing at a time.
6. Write down your problems and duties on a slip of paper before going to sleep—get them out of your mind and down on paper.
7. Take vacations, "breakations" (short mini-vacations), recreation and naps when you need them.

Remember, you can be very creative — if you can just get yourself out of the way!

5

HAPPINESS IS A HABIT

THE MIND
CAN CURE ITSELF

If we can learn to relax, the subconscious is released from worry and tension and immediately sets about healing itself. A physical wound will heal itself quite quickly if you will give it proper attention and then leave it alone. The mind also has a way of healing itself since the success mechanism has a continuous built-in striving for happiness and success.

Good ideas are like medicine and vitamins for the mind. But, just as medicines and vitamins only assist the body in a job it is already doing, the main curative processes occur spontaneously and naturally. However, we often hinder the healing process by constantly picking at our mental, emotional, and physical hurts and sores as well as those of others. When we relax and accept ourselves, we allow the real world to reach us and we can begin to find life very interesting and rich in detail. When this happens and we quit dwelling on ourselves, our mind gets busy and will cure itself.

STRESS HURTS

Stress definitely hurts and it can handicap the happiness habit. Kids used to play a game at night and sing, "Ain't no buggers out tonight, Poppa shot 'em all last night." This song gave the confidence to venture into dark and scary hiding places where they really didn't want to go alone.

Most of us fight the "stress bugger" and he is vicious. In 1982, the American Academy of Family Physicians stated that 66 percent of all medical problems were directly related to stress.

Ulcers are not caused by what you eat — they are caused by what's eating you!

Worry, tension, headaches, rashes, ulcers, hypertension, heart attacks and even accidents can all come from stress.

What exactly is stress? Stress is your body's attempt to adjust to pressure or change. Pressure comes from outside forces. Stress is the internal effect.

Millions of dollars are being spent each year on medical research to determine how we can cope most effectively with stress. We'll be talking more about this later, but for now, let's focus on one method that researchers, physicians and psychiatrists all agree helps — **relaxation**.

William James was able to cite example after example of people who had tried unsuccessfully for years to rid themselves of anxieties, worries, and feelings of inferiority and guilt. By making continuous conscious efforts to be free of them, they struggled and failed. Yet they found that success finally came when they gave up the conscious struggle and stopped trying to solve their problems by thinking about them. James said, "Relaxation, not intentness, should now be the rule. Give up the feeling of responsibility, let go of yourself, resign the care of your destiny to higher powers, and be genuinely indifferent as to what becomes of it all — it is but giving your private compulsive self a rest, and finding that a greater self is there. The results remain firm facts of human nature."

THE FIRST STEP
TOWARD HAPPINESS

In his book, <u>Man In Search of Meaning,</u> Dr. Viktor Frankl, says that people who try to push their way through the door to happiness are certain to fail. The door to happiness opens inward and the harder you push against it, the more it closes on you. Even the very gesture of stopping at a door, gripping the handle, and then pulling inward and stepping back reveals the emotional and physical posture necessary for any of us if we are to be happy. We must open ourselves to others, to life, and to reality. This relaxed newness makes life pleasurable, interesting, and exciting. We feel everyone would be happy if all of life were that way.

From the beginning of this text we have stressed that all of us react to life based upon our positive or negative self-concept. This means that we do not respond to facts as they are, but to facts as they appear to us or facts as they affect us. Even good things can have an unpleasant effect on people with a negative self-concept. We can go to a beautiful new housing development, well planned, neat, fully equipped, tastefully designed and so on, but dislike the whole thing because most of the lawns are still mud or because we found two shaky bannisters. Comments will be negative: "Boy, they just throw up a piece of garbage these days and then charge you a fortune for it. They are so eager to sell this junk, they can't even wait for the area to look presentable before they start trying to push it." Somewhere along the way, we have all been guilty of this kind of unhappy behavior and petty negativism. As long as you react to life this way, then happiness is impossible. But the real problem is what do you think of yourself ? Your reactions will be based upon your self-concept.

This brings us to the main point. Happiness is a state of mind wherein, your thoughts and reactions are pleasant most of the time. This means that happiness should be a habit. It is a habit you must form and establish as one of your virtues.

From this simple idea, a few other ideas flow naturally. For one, success does not cause happiness, but it is the other way around. **Happiness precedes and causes success.**

Suicide among those who are considered wealthy or well to do is not uncommon. This could lead us to believe it is more important to be happy than rich.

To illustrate the point: A wealthy executive sitting in an exclusive club one evening, revealed to another executive that he was in the process of being divorced by his wife, had alienated his children, was bitterly lonely, and had no goal or purpose in his life. In his haste to get rich he had lost his ability to live, feel, and enjoy the things that really mattered most to him. Unfortunately, he didn't analyze his true priorities until it was too late to recover with the people he really cared about.

Happiness is not something that happens to you, but must be learned. Happiness is not to be confused with pleasure. **You can buy pleasure, but you must achieve happiness. Happiness isn't for sale.**

HAPPINESS IS NOW

People may have rather dull lives with only spots of brightness. Consequently, these people are usually unhappy or negative in their attitude most of the time. They possess sporadic happiness, meaning they are happy for a few episodes a year, but the major theme of their lives is negative or unhappy. These people reinforce this tendency by thinking, "I'll be happy when I change jobs" or, "I'll be happy when I get a raise."

Consider another example of how we attach happiness to things and experiences yet to come. There are people who always seem to think the grass is greener elsewhere. When they're at home, they can't wait for vacation time to come. When on vacation they say, "I can't wait to get home, unpack, and get back to our routine." During the year they long for the holidays. During holidays they don't like the pace. In the car they can't wait to arrive at their destination, so they rush so much they never enjoy the trip. They don't like their current job, but think they'll love the next one and plan to work harder once they get it.

Know anyone like this? Hopefully, you don't see him or her every time you look in the mirror.

We are not born happy — it is learned. **Happiness is achieved in the here and now, not in some distant place or some future date.**

Happiness is either now or it is forever in front of you somewhere, sometime. Thinking that you will be happy someday quickly becomes an attitude or emotional habit, and you walk through your whole life chasing the rainbow of happiness.

Does this sound familiar? Have you ever caught yourself saying, "I'll be happier when...?" If those words sound like you, watch out! This means you have a pattern of looking to the future for your emotional contentment. Now is the time for you to enjoy. You can't enjoy tomorrow until it gets here.

A little girl named Lisa did much the same thing. Lisa was an insecure child who was always looking for something or someone to make her happy. Her parents were frequently hard with her and then felt guilty afterwards and over indulged her with gifts and toys. She lived her life divided between tears and ecstasy, with very little normal contentment in between.

At a birthday party given in her honor, she didn't want to play games with her guests because she was looking forward to the snacks and candy. When she began to withdraw and pout, her mother broke up the games early to get to the refreshments. As soon as she started eating, she became worried about the cake and wouldn't eat anything until the candles were lit and the ice cream was served. She never finished her cake, though, because she insisted that she open her presents. She opened the largest first and rushed through package after package. She tore open the last package, looked around at all the children with a strange bewilderment, and started to cry. She had nothing more to look forward to. It was suddenly over.

Many of us do the same thing by always putting happiness a little in front of us, instead of enjoying what we have NOW! Happiness is not something that comes to you because you are good. We must put forth a conscious effort and work toward being happy, because it would not be understood or appreciated if it were just handed to us.

HAPPINESS AND RELATIONSHIPS

Have you ever wondered why the divorce rate is so high? Happiness obviously is a factor — or at least the lack of happiness. Good relationships take hard work. Too many people do not enter into a relationship understanding that it takes this conscious effort and work to make us and others happy. Wouldn't it be great if we could just sit back and let our spouse do all the work, all the giving and all of the making us happy? Sorry, but it just doesn't work that way. You have to work at it too. No one else has an obligation to make you happy. You have to give yourself happiness — you can't "take" it from others. Amazingly, it is easiest to find for ourselves when we are working to give it to others. Try it. Put out effort to please someone else. The minute you succeed and see them enjoying your efforts, take a mental snapshot of yourself. That photograph will show you a happy person — yourself. The point is this — **you get happiness by giving happiness.**

Jake, one of our students in a personal development class, when asked by the instructor what he was going to do on the weekend, replied, "I'm going to goof off and do nothing and maybe take the children out while their mother is gone. The instructor asked, "Where is she?"

Jake replied, " She's going to her baptism."

"Aren't you going with her?" the instructor questioned.

"No," was the answer, "She is joining this stupid sect that I don't believe in and I want no part of it. They believe in so and so and she can just lead her own life. She believes so strongly and I can't get her to change."

"Do you love her?" he was asked.

"Yes"

"Do you intend to stay married or get a divorce?"

"We want to stay married, but things are bad because of this."

"Isn't it possible that you could be wrong? After all, she believes something strongly and you've tried every way to change her. Is that the most awful belief in the world?"

"No, I guess not, but she won't change and I can't accept her concepts."

"Maybe, you could change what you can accept. Maybe you can give her the privilege of her own concepts. Who says you can't give? If she were Republican and you were Democrat, would you refuse to drive her to the polling place?"

"No," he replied.

Two days later he said he would go with her to the baptism. A week later he said things had really smoothed out. He didn't agree with her philosophy, but he and his wife were much closer because she appreciated his efforts. He gave happiness and it is paying off.

Spinoza made his great contribution to Western thought: "Happiness is not the reward of being virtuous but is virtue itself." We are not happy because we control our animal nature, but on the contrary, because we are happy, we are able to control it. So being good or virtuous will not make you happy, but being happy leads to kindness, generosity and discipline.

For instance, Ned had a terrible time controlling his tendencies to oversleep, overeat, and act and think negatively. He seemed to feel unhappy most of the time.

Through study, and a helpful companion, he realized that he was basically a fine person — curious, willing to concede and generally quick to learn. Gradually, he developed a self-understanding and self-image which allowed him to worry less. As he became more relaxed, cheerful, and developed the courage to be himself, he found that work became challenging, that he didn't want to oversleep, that he was less negative as he accepted the truth about himself and others, and that he now pursued things with sincerity and real interest.

He said, "I've been trying to discipline myself for years. What I really needed was to take care of my basic needs for self-respect and self-confidence. Once I started to accept and believe in my own worth, the vicious tendencies I thought I had just sort of melted away without too much attention to them." In Ned's case, happiness became a virtue. **Seeking happiness is not selfish; it is a duty.**

YOU ACTUALLY
NEED PROBLEMS

People think that they would be happy if they didn't have any problems. Problems are part of life itself. The only people without problems are dead. Actually, happiness is not possible without some conflict to act as a catalyst and gauge.

In the case of Harry, the need for conflict became apparent after the third year of what appeared to be a dream marriage. To understand more clearly Harry's situation, we must know something of Harry's background. Harry was raised in an impoverished, negative atmosphere. This caused him to leave home at an early age. With great desire and determination, Harry set himself to the task of completing high school and college all on his own. During this time of working his way through school, Harry set a goal to earn thirty thousand dollars a year. To Harry this would have been the pinnacle of success.

In his senior year of college, Harry fell in love and was married. It was at that time that Harry's problem began. He found that his wife was able to get a forty thousand dollar a year job.

Harry's goal had been thirty thousand dollars a year for so long that it was difficult for him to adjust to his new, second level status. He became resentful and unhappy and began to feel insecure and developed a lack of direction. It was necessary for him to seek psychiatric guidance and make a conscious effort to re-establish practical goals. It was discovered that his wife's job had served only as an instrument of personal self-destruction and ego deflation for Harry. It had robbed his need to push himself.

Harry is now living a happier life, with involvement in his own business. He accepted his wife's success. He is now experiencing challenges and conflict and has afforded himself the opportunity of a full life.

We hear people all around us say, "I want my children to have it better than I did." The next step is to start giving them things— material things — A car or a life insurance policy to leave them a half million dollars when we die. We help them solve their problems or fight their battles for them. What happens? We take away all of the chances for a person to grow.

We grow from the way we respond to obstacles. The worst thing that can happen is to remove all of the obstacles. We can be lulled into thinking that by giving material things we help the individual. The child needs the intangible things, many of which only he or she can earn. We can give, love, care, etc. A child earns diligence, stamina, courage, and the multitude of other desirable qualities. They need to solve their own problems and face their own obstacles. Of course, we can back them up and be there when they need support. Intangibles can often be gained by having to work for the tangibles. Lavish material goods on the children, and in turn you may take away some of the means of stretching and growing.

Happiness does not depend on externals. Even the most active and wealthy life can be basically meaningless and unhappy. This statement, made by a reigning monarch, is one of the most beautiful yet sad statements on this subject. It expresses the dilemma of the man who thinks that things, people, or possessions will make him happy. It's a serious mistake and it has no remedy.

> "I have now reigned for more than fifty years, loved by my subjects, dreaded by my enemies, and respected by my allies. Riches and honors, power and pleasure, have waited on my call—nor does any earthly blessing appear to have been wanting to my felicity. In this situation I have diligently numbered the days of pure and genuine happiness which have fallen to my lot: They amount to fourteen."

This illustrates the point that money, power, honor, titles, etc. simply do not a happy person make.

A psychologist, Dr. Matthew M. Chappell, said, "Happiness is purely internal. It is produced not by objects, but by an attitude which can be developed and constructed by the individual's own activities, irrespective of his environment." Happiness is good medicine and we function better when we are happy.

THE POWER
OF HAPPINESS

When you are happy, memory improves, you see more acutely, your hearing is better, food tastes better, ideas flow more abundantly, and you feel more energetic.

Unhappiness, on the other hand, literally causes sickness. Many forms of disease are just that, "dis — ease," discomfort, distress — unhappiness. Some of the most common diseases are caused by unhappiness or our inability to adjust to pressure — stress, as we mentioned earlier.

Just as happiness is a habit, we should also point out that **unhappiness is a habit**. It is a skill that most of us picked up easily and have virtually perfected. Very early in life we learned that all we had to do was to get unhappy enough and others would give us attention. This created a habit which can prompt us to react to many things with unhappiness, dissatisfaction and hurt. Many people easily manipulate their friends or family members by pulling a "hurt" act. Statements like, "You just don't like me anymore" are typical of this type of person. Those reactions and feelings are quickly taken up by our system as ways to get what we want, and we unconsciously carry them right through to adult life. When they begin to create havoc, we sometimes wonder what's wrong with us. Nothing is wrong. We have simply developed the "wrong" habits.

If you are ever going to be happy, you might as well resign yourself to Lincoln's old adage: **"Most people are about as happy as they make up their minds to be."** We need to be able to stop being emotionally manipulated by external forces, people and conditions. It is your right to be happy and you can form the habit. You don't need to be unhappy.

6

HOW TO OUTWIT FAILURE

HANDLING UNHAPPINESS

Just as happiness precedes and causes success, usually unhappiness precedes and causes failure. Just as happiness is learned, so is unhappiness. As we stated earlier, unhappiness is an emotional habit.

Since unhappiness is so destructive, we should look at the symptoms of unhappiness and failure. Then we can understand them, avoid them, and generally outwit them. Let's talk about the symptoms of the failure prone personality and try to see how it is caused and how it reinforces a poor self-image.

First, recognize that **everyone feels unhappy from time to time.** When you are down in the dumps, you're by no means alone. Most unstable personalities, when seeking professional psychiatric assistance, think they are the only ones who have felt so hopeless or who have ever done such horrible things. Fortunately they are wrong. Any one of us can, and usually does, experience such feelings.

In the unhealthy personality, negative emotions, fear, hatred, anxiety ,and guilt are felt just as strongly, or even more strongly, than in the healthy personalities. The healthy personality also suffers these feelings, but over appropriate situations and not for too long a period of time. Everybody has these negative feelings, and they are necessary and vital ones. They should not, however, rule our lives.

To illustrate how these feelings can be controlled, we are reminded of a sales manager named Howard. Howard was known as an unusually enthusiastic and dynamic sales manager who had a sharp, quick wit. His salesforce admired him, and his success in many areas was widely recognized. One day the president of his company walked into his office and Howard obviously looked bad. His boss commented that it was unusual to see "Mr. Cheer" looking like "Mr. Blue." Howard looked up at his boss, grinned tiredly, pushed back his chair, and said, "Don, it's crazy, but I get these periods now and then when I feel a lot of doubt about my abilities, and I feel guilty about duties imperfectly performed. I think a great deal and I do a lot of reading. When I finally do run across an idea that changes my mood, I'm genuinely enthusiastic. That's why the ideas that I teach to others come across, I suppose. These occasional weak periods keep me learning, keep me humble and make me think. Often, it is just the sense of relief when doubt subsides, that makes me enthusiastic. I've always accepted my negative moods because they provide the dark that makes the light real light. This sounds corny, I suppose, but it is real for me."

We all have these feelings, only most of us fear them and hate them. We can learn to handle, manage, and live through these feelings as Howard did. His reflection on his moods and his willingness to simply accept them as moods that will pass, shows resilience. **Resilience, the ability to bounce back, is an excellent attribute to develop.**

RECOGNIZING
THE SYMPTOMS OF FAILURE

Fear of Failure: This may be the biggest crippler of all. The fear of failing can cause you to freeze-up at critical moments. It can cause hives, indigestion, fainting spells, dizziness and all kinds of other physical symptoms.

Perhaps the worst effect of fear of failure, however, is that it can keep you from even trying. This symptom is especially devastating because it is hard to identify. Jim said he would always wait until the last minute to study for tests in college and settle for a grade of C. His roommate would comment that he didn't understand how Jim could do it. Only years later did Jim realize that what he was really doing was padding himself against failure. He said "If I had ever said I was going to study and make an A and then only made a B, I would have failed to make my goal." By not studying and not trying, it was impossible to fail to meet the goal — especially since one had not been set. Fear crippled his effort.

Emptiness: This is boredom, tiredness, tastelessness, and the "so what" feeling. This symptom is a defense mechanism caused by many disappointments. By not caring at all, at least we don't suffer the lash of additional disappointment. The person who is suffering from emptiness and boredom usually strangles off his good impulses and desires as soon as they come to the surface. It is an inappropriate response to problems and disappointments because after awhile all life becomes blah. It cuts down our eagerness and curiosity, and when that is gone, we cannot see that life is valuable.

Guilt: Guilt is a deep cause for unhappiness. It comes from actual or imagined wrong doing or faults. Some guilt is all right as long as it makes you change. However, it can be destructive if it lingers. Prolonged and chronic guilt, causes depression, fault finding or condemnation of others and self. Guilt can be the result of not seeing all the facts that go into our behavior. It is reinforced by invoking absolute standards, other people's standards, or measuring ourselves against perfection. **Prolonged guilt means we cannot give ourselves the gift of forgiving and forgetting.**

Guilt is very much associated with ethics and morals, right and wrong. Some guilt is acceptable, but a chronic sense of guilt is unacceptable.

The following example illustrates the extent to which such feelings manifest themselves. Joe was the type of person who tended to harbor many guilt feelings. One of the things that bothered him most was his habit of smoking. He felt it was self-punishing, expensive, stupid and dangerous. Every cancer ad cut through him like a knife.

One day Joe encountered an old friend who was a professor in sociology. As they talked, the professor took out a cigarette and lit it up. As Joe lit a cigarette for himself, he had feelings of guilt and expressed these to his friend. The other man looked at him and casually remarked, "I've had this fondness for tobacco for years, just as I like potato chips and Coca-Cola. I kind of expect these things in myself." It impressed Joe how the other man seemed so good natured about his weakness and felt much less guilty.

Over the next few weeks Joe admitted his fondness for tobacco and began to notice how the force of habit affected his own life and the lives of other people. He began to understand how they got that way. He decided to smoke only if he wanted to and, to his surprise, he found out that by smoking only when he really wanted to, he smoked much less. Soon one pack lasted him about four days. He started some excellent breathing and physical exercises which helped him to relax and reduce his stress and the desire for smoking. He took control of the habit instead of letting it control him.

Anxiety: Tension causes unhappiness. Anxiety is that constant overattention to self and life, which is often based on the feeling that things may not work out. The overly anxious person often may see himself as a likely loser and can be anxious over everything. Any little loss just forebodes greater and more disastrous losses. The anxious person is often hurried, rude, tired and easily angered.

On the positive side, however, this anxiety, when properly controlled, can cause a person to push extra hard, take extra care, and perform at a high level.

Tom was one of those anxious people, always in a hurry to get what he wanted. One of the ways (among many others) that it affected him was in his driving. It was costing him about eighty-five a year for minor speeding tickets. He realized one day that his speeding was caused by anxiety and his anxiety was reinforced every time he was stopped by the police.

Tom has finally learned to coast along, enjoy the sights, his car, the radio, his driving skill, and even help other motorists whenever he gets the chance. When he drives, he knows he can't do anything concrete about any of his problems, so he relaxes. Now he arrives refreshed and in good humor. He also experiences many ideas while he's driving and keeps a tape recorder on the seat of his car so that he won't lose any of his ideas. Tom defeated this anxiety by learning to enjoy the trip.

Closed-Mindedness: This is often a symptom of the failure prone personality or a person who is afraid to be wrong. It is caused by the idea that we must always be right — that to be wrong would destroy the only ego-ideal we can accept, the absolute or perfect self. The closed-minded person will go to great lengths to prove his position correct.

These people are inclined to say, "You didn't tell me so, or I would have done it" or, "Not all the information was available." They simply have a really tough time admitting their mistakes. He or she is often a miserable person because he cannot accept the real, fallible, genuine self.

Egocentricity: Thinking about oneself all the time is an indicator of this characteristic. This can be a terrible prison wherein one is always conscious of his every act, desire, emotion, need and feeling. The egocentric person still sees himself or herself as dependent upon life to make him happy. All decisions are made based on what "I" want to do, never to give to or serve others. He has not recognized, as yet, that **life is not for the go-getters. It is for the go-givers.** The egocentric person basically considers himself special and different. He needs everything because he is getting nothing from himself but contempt.

Uncertainty: The uncertain person can see himself or herself as uninformed and confused. As such, he wants too much to be right.

Rather than go ahead and make a decision and risk being wrong, **he decides not to decide** and makes no decision at all. This keeps him frozen in fear of error. By never making decisions, he hopes to clear up his indecision. These people over-plan and under-act. People who go through life hoping that nothing happens, experience just that — **Nothing!** The indecisive person procrastinates forever so he does not get the chance to seize the ideas, the people, and the opportunities that could change his life. This person must learn to force himself to take action and quit hesitating.

Resentment: Resentment is a deadly poison. It uses human energy in great amounts. Resentment makes you feel morally superior to others by hating them and blaming them. As a slave for the ego, resentment is a cure worse than the disease that caused it. It is generally derived from a guilty conscience and from the feeling that others make you feel a particular way. Only you can make yourself feel a particular way. You are responsible for your own feelings. **Since the resentful person blames his feelings on the actions of others**, he is still emotionally dependent and basically lacks self-reliance.

Emotional Instability: This also causes unhappiness which can lead to failure. By this we are talking about strong swings in a person's behavior from very positive, enthusiastic and cheerful one day, to despondent, grumpy and full of self-doubt the next. All of us experience some swings in our feelings and emotions, but when these swings become too strong, we should try to control our reactions a little more. This might mean curbing our enthusiasm on the one hand and learning to maintain our sense of humor on the other. It is very easy to allow yourself to dwell on the negatives and get "bent out of shape" unnecessarily. We should recognize, however, that in cases where these emotional swings are severe, there may exist a condition called "manic depressive." The "manic depressive" has a chemical imbalance which may be treated with medication.

Loneliness: This is a deep unhappiness. It is caused by alienation and a lack of oneness with self and others. The lonely person cannot accept others, so he or she finds fault with them beforehand, withdraws from them even further and deepens his loneliness.

Loneliness is overcome by forcing yourself to mix and mingle with people. After awhile you may find yourself getting so busy and occupied that you forget the loneliness. Once your real personality actually shows through to people, people will like and respond to you.

Here is how one person conquered her loneliness. Melinda was not a pretty child, but that was only the smallest part of her problem. She was epileptic. Her parents were shocked and scared when Melinda had her first seizure at age seven. They were embarrassed and tried to keep the whole thing quiet and, in so doing, developed an atmosphere of secrecy and guilt around the girl. She felt guilty and ashamed for something she had absolutely no control over. She attended school and did well, but everyone knew she was "different" and avoided her. Obviously, she was quite lonely and it was hardly a surprise when, at age fourteen, she eloped with a sixteen year-old.

Marriage did not solve her loneliness problem, and the two youngsters put up with many relocations, little income and no permanent friends. As their fortunes declined, they moved to lower income and more impoverished neighborhoods.

Finally, in a migrant labor camp, Melinda discovered herself and accepted the fact that she had good qualities to offer. *(Are you getting closer to the secret for success?)* Here's the way it happened with Melinda. Another migrant came to her with a letter one day, asking her to read it for him because he couldn't read. It was almost the first time that anyone had ever really needed her help. She gladly read the letter and then asked if the man intended to reply. He said that he might if he could get someone to write it. Melinda said she would do it. This simple act resulted in her working with seven adults that summer, teaching them how to read and write. Today she is a therapeutic teacher for children with reading problems. She hasn't been lonely for years and her life has purpose and direction.

To get over loneliness one must **seize opportunities to get involved with people.**

The worst thing that we can do with these feelings is hate them and hide from them. Many of these feelings are, as we stated earlier, caused or magnified by a poor self-image or a lack of confidence. **One of the fastest cures for sagging confidence is to focus your attraction on helping someone else. You can't concentrate on yourself and someone else simultaneously.**

CONTROLLING YOUR EMOTIONS

Psychologists and physicians have discovered that unexpressed emotions negatively affect the mind and body of the individual restricting them. Emotions are powerful forces that need to be released in some way; they must have an outlet. For that reason, psychologists point out that **good emotional control is maintained by experiencing our emotions** and allowing them to go through their natural processes. Let's look at this a little closer.

Let's say that you start to sense a feeling of guilt. Most of us stop, hold in, or repress the feeling of guilt and force ourselves to relax, or work, or otherwise keep on going. Don't forget that when we feel things, we must feel them somewhere within ourselves. Lots of us feel guilt in the pit of our stomach. It may churn, burn, or make us feel nauseous. In order to quit feeling guilty, you try to ignore these messages from the stomach, but many other feelings are also experienced in the stomach, such as excitement, warmth, and peace. By ignoring your guilt feelings, you can be ignoring all messages from it, good and bad. Consequently, our effort to strangle off the one emotion can cause such tension in that area that you develop an ulcer, chronic nausea, touchy digestion or heartburn. Rather than choke off emotions like the ones we have described, turn these enemies into friends. Experience them.

Guilt is a good example because the emotional sequence set off by guilt is so clear-cut. Normally, if a person "fully experiences" his guilt, he then feels a bit sick and disgusted. This makes him angry with himself. People who feel guilt often repent and determine to live better. People who repress their guilt and never experience it, never really feel the full impact of their wrong doing and may harbor their guilt for years while it slowly eats away at them.

A lady in her late seventies tearfully told her son, "I just hope you never find out some of the things I've thought or done over the years." She was totally distraught. Her health has been failing and she has suffered significant memory loss. After a thorough medical evaluation, the doctor indicated that she seems to be allowing some long-harbored guilt to literally destroy her health and her memory.

You may need to experience these emotions, all by yourself, or perhaps you may wish to confide in a friend. If you feel and experience resentment, for example, you may find yourself yelling at the top of your lungs or crying. While it's courteous to do that sort of thing alone, a scene like that may also clearly point out to you your childishness, the depth of your hurt, and the way you let others control you. It can leave you feeling relieved, a little embarrassed, honestly able to face the truth and much more calm.

An individual named Steve, from North Carolina, told us in a class that he has a favorite tree stump on his property. Steve says he can go out to that stump, away from everyone, late in the afternoon, and just "sort of reflect on my feelings." He indicated that on occasions he may holler and scream, cry, or just sit and pout. This may sound silly to you, but remember this — **inside everyone of us, just barely beneath the surface, is a two year old just dying to get out and pitch a fit**. Every now and then, in the right circumstances, it might be smart to allow the two year old to run free for a little while.

We are not suggesting that you fully experience every little emotion that you have. We are suggesting that you get to know your real feelings by allowing them to be experienced and lived. When you give yourself permission to experience your negative emotions, let the rational, conscious part of your mind observe the emotion that you feel. When everything has leveled out again, you can talk to yourself and evaluate the situation. **People who live through their emotions know they can take it**. They faced it, they felt it, they lived through it. It is completed. There's even a feeling of accomplishment when it is over.

Remember, your physical system will always work toward health. If you allow your system to work, then it will strive automatically to bring you to a healthy state. Loneliness experienced can lead to self-pity and whining. Whining can lead to incredibly ridiculous charges and complaints. These complaints are often so ridiculous that we end up laughing at ourselves. People who laugh aren't lonely.

The symptoms of unhappiness and failure cease to bother us as much if we take them in stride, knowing we can work through them and come out all right on the other side. But notice that each successive emotion must be "fully" experienced. You can't stop the process just because you don't want to go any further.

In other words, **we outwit failure by simply refusing to be scared of it.**

7

TURN FAILURE INTO SUCCESS

UNDERSTANDING YOUR ENEMIES

In the previous chapter we discussed the symptoms of the failure prone personality. There are many others, but the list we discussed will do for a start.

Somehow we must recognize that all the foregoing personality characteristics, attitudes, and reactions cause unhappiness and unhappiness breeds failure. These human reactions can lose their repulsive quality only when we can understand their evolution within our own personality and see them for what they are — not necessarily bad, just "inappropriate."

These characteristics of personality: fearfulness, guilt, boredom, loneliness, resentment, etc., fight against our happiness and self-acceptance and can make our lives truly unhappy. Understand that anything that wars against you is an "enemy." These are the enemies of the human spirit. A young man in Palestine some two thousand years ago, gave us a wonderful clue, "Love your enemies." And that is just what we have to do with the human conflict we discussed in the last chapter. We have to understand, accept with good humor, and handle gently all those emotions, whether they happen to occur within ourselves or within others. If you can accept the way you feel and behave, then you can accept anybody's feelings and behavior. By accepting and understanding your behavior, you will relax and begin to face situations with others more openly and honestly.

A young lady named Gwen Lowe, in one of our classes, told of an experience that made her wrestle with her emotional enemies, examine and accept her behavior. Her mother was a severe alcoholic by the time Gwen was twelve years old, and Gwen had to take over most of the household duties for the family. Eventually her mother refused to even allow the kids to put up a Christmas tree or decorate for holidays. When Gwen was eighteen she moved out and promptly dismissed her past life by telling everyone that her mother was deceased. For five years, resentment and hatred dominated her life. Finally she began to accept the fact that her resentment was natural and she realized that she really did, in fact, love her mother. She just missed the mother who loved her as a small child and hated what the alcohol had done to her. Having put the problem in proper perspective, she then committed her mother for involuntary treatment. It hurt her terribly to do this to her mother. She knew, however, that she'd made the correct choice when late that year, on Christmas morning, she pulled into her mother's driveway and saw a gorgeous Christmas tree in the front window! Gwen said, "I knew my real mother had finally come home!"

It all started off by her realization that she was her own worst enemy, not her mother. She had to realize that the barrier was not only the alcohol but her resentment. **Once the resentment was put in perspective, she could realistically help her mother tackle the alcohol problem.**

ACCEPTING YOUR ENEMIES

We must not fight the symptoms of failure. We must not hate ourselves or others with those feelings. Those feelings have many deep underlying causes. People aren't hateful just because it is their nature. They are just hurting, despairing, and confused. They simply have developed the habit of reacting that way and often do not even realize it. Most "bad" people are good people who are in trouble with themselves. We see only the surface, their defensive front, rather than the true human spirit and the struggle underneath.

People put up defenses and fronts like conceit, boredom, and ugliness to protect their sagging ego. Inside they are good and wholesome individuals. Here is an example of one such defense.

Gary was a salesman who grated on his customer's nerves by talking very loud, swaggering, and being flip. He forgot that his purpose was to sell, not to entertain, not to act macho, and not to act cute. Many people regarded him as a bore and were often offended by his boisterous manners. Later, he acknowledged that he really felt scared and inferior to other people. The bravado was an act. Gary had the courage to apologize to many of his customers after he was able to accept the truth about himself and drop his facade. Most of them accepted his honesty and his attempt to change his offensive behavior. From then on Gary got along with people in a much more friendly and sincere way.

Often we are inclined to look at the person in the room who is the center of attention and think he or she has all the confidence in the world. In fact, the opposite could be true. He may be the most insecure person around and is fighting a battle to conquer his fears.

Somehow we must come to accept these things in ourselves and others with as little repulsion and as much openness and understanding as we can. This brings us to one of the most misunderstood of all human abilities, the ability to accept — to give in and be passive, instead of fighting.

Passivity is not properly understood in our active and fast paced society. Giving in, accepting and forgiving, is generally regarded as a weakness. However, just the opposite can be true. To hang on and on, to refuse to budge, is a form of fear, terror, weakness and self-doubt. It takes tremendous strength, courage, humor, ultimate optimism and confidence to let go — to laugh and shrug your shoulders good naturedly.

Think back to when you were a kid and got into one of those, "Did so!" "Did not!" "Did too so!" "No, I didn't!" type of arguments. Worse yet, they usually occurred in front of your friends. Both sides were scared of losing face. Many relationships have been threatened or damaged by this lack of confidence that forced us not to give in. Unfortunately, most of us never really grow completely out of that stage. We just get a little more subtle than shouting, "Did so!" "Did not!" **Too many relationships are still being damaged every day by people who refuse to give in to another person.**

Passivity can sometimes be the most beautiful of all human strengths, and its power can at times bring tears to the most callous and sophisticated eyes. Acceptance is not weak! It is true greatness when handled appropriately.

IDENTIFYING YOURSELF IN OTHERS

Usually we don't enjoy being around people whose lives are made dark or painful by their own tensions, angers, resentments, fears and despairs. They simply make life unpleasant for everyone. Most often these individuals are not entirely mature. Underneath they may be scared and lonely. A psychiatrist said, "You can tell a lot about a person's character and personality by the way he reacts to children." The psychiatrist who made this statement knew very well what he was talking about. If you reject and abhor children because of their actions and feelings, then you will probably hate and despise yourself when you demonstrate similar, "childish" behavior. In fact, research has now shown that you can easily "hate" those people who remind you of the "real" you. You may now see why you dislike some people. As much as you hate to admit it, the faults and flaws they have, the areas that drive you up the wall, are probably some of the same faults you also have. It is simply easier to despise them in someone else than to "hate" yourself.

For example, a friend of ours commented one day, "I consider myself to be lazy in many ways, even though no one else I know would call me lazy. Insofar as work is concerned, I churn out a tremendous amount. As far as family or community activities are concerned, I stay busy. Exercise, on the other hand, is something I just never seem to get around to doing — no matter how many times I urge myself to do it. Consequently, I find myself almost wanting to cut early morning joggers down with my car because I resent the self-discipline they have. Their self-discipline makes me feel guilty."

We all have these negative feelings. Now we must learn to accept, understand and even "love" these feelings within ourselves. If we dwell on them, they seem to multiply. If we fight them, they give us ulcers. If we ignore them and pretend they don't exist, they loom large in the darker corners of our mind and sneak out when least expected. If we attack them, they flee from us or overwhelm us. **We simply have to recognize them as our feelings, understand them, accept them, and gently learn from them.**

OVERCOMING
"ENEMY" BAD TRAITS

You cannot overcome unpleasant characteristics in yourself or others by force or criticism. People act badly because some deep basic needs are not satisfied. Until these needs are satisfied, they will have a poor self-image and behavior problems usually result.

Here is an example of how force proved unsuccessful. Bill tried to force his wife, children and others into being honest and thoughtful. He criticized their double motives, revealed their carelessness and selfishness, and constantly reminded them of their responsibilities. To avoid his badgering, they began to lie to him. As time went on, even friends wouldn't do a single thoughtful thing for him. He was crushed.

Someone finally suggested to him that perhaps he was the one who was wrong and apologized. If he were to be the leader, he would have to change tactics. So Bill practiced being honest and thoughtful himself. He admitted to them that he was wrong and apologized. He became honest with himself and tried to make them feel good, loved and understood instead of criticized, exposed and rejected. Bill didn't overcome the "enemy" in himself or in his family by resentment, hatred or force. He accepted and overcame it with good. He did not return dislike for dislike but accepted his own responsibility, swallowed his pride, and did the right thing by apologizing.

HIDING BEHIND A FACADE

The people who frequently feel the unhappiness we have been discussing have learned to feel this way from thousands of hurts, injuries, and disappointments. Their self-image is badly scarred and to themselves they appear ugly. They cannot accept themselves and are certain that others cannot either. They then either put up a workable front or quit trying altogether. Behind the phony front or facade and the wall behind which we would withdraw and quit altogether, are fear, hostility, resentment, and callousness.

Often we feel that we are the only person who has suffered all these hurts, disappointments, setbacks and injuries. We look at others and think they have all the luck. In his book, Peace of Mind, Rabbi Joshua Liebman says (and we paraphrase here), **"If you and I could see the scars of others from all the battles they fought and lost, our own scars would weigh less heavy."** What he is telling us is to quit feeling sorry for ourselves. Everyone has suffered. Recognize that every basic and real personality is unique and has many beautiful aspects. To defeat your personal "enemy traits" you must first learn to be yourself and drop the facades.

In one of our classes, an executive named Rob had to come to grips with his real personality and drop his facade. Managers from all over the country were together in the seminar. During the week several people told us there was absolutely no way they would ever work for Rob. He was too "phony," they said. Later Rob commented to the instructor that we really didn't understand leadership, that his secret was to maintain a facade and never really let his people get to know him. He actually used the word "facade." Remember, that means "false front." The instructor passed on to Rob the fact that several people in the class had not been impressed with his facade and said they would never work for him. This feedback cut him to the bone. The next day, after a rather sleepless night, Rob apologized to the group and said he had suddenly learned the value of being genuine. **Facades simply don't fool people for very long.**

Most of us are continually wondering and worrying what people will think of us and say about us. Be true to yourself and if you interpret the actions of others in a good and healthy light, and if you actively like, accept and encourage them first, they will eventually think well of you.

The following is a good example of this important concept. The President of a large American company on the verge of bankruptcy had a novel idea for advertising. Everyone thought that he was a stupid idealist to even think of it. The Board of Directors vetoed the idea and personal animosities arose. Interestingly enough, it was the President alone who maintained a positive and understanding attitude toward everyone else, while the others exemplified hostility. Over a period of eight months he talked individually with all of the board members and gradually swung them around to his way of thinking. The advertising program was a huge success, one of the most outstanding in the history of American advertising. People were impressed by the new image that the ads created, and the company emerged from its financial difficulty. Today the company continues the same advertising program and the President maintains the same actively positive attitude toward others regardless of their attitude toward him.

THE GREATEST SUCCESS

Such a change, the miracle of turning failure or hardship into success, or taking the unacceptable self and learning to like it, is a tremendous human achievement. It opens the way to understanding and acceptance of others. Recognize, however, that this type of change may take time. **Virtually any change to self or to your behavior comes very slowly, very painfully, and in very small increments.** With this attitude, the world becomes a friendly place, indeed, loaded with all sorts of possibilities.

Our failures or hardships can sometimes be the very things that cause us to succeed. Consider Arthur Gray who attended one of our seminars. He told of his delight when his daughter was born and of his fear of losing his family forever when he was drafted and sent to Vietnam. His worst nightmares were almost realized when he stepped on a homemade booby trap. The explosion almost killed him and severely damaged his legs. For two years he vegetated in the V.A. hospital feeling sorry for himself and didn't even want his family to see him crippled and in a wheelchair. His weight dropped to ninety-eight pounds. Finally, his little daughter got through to him when she cried and said, "I don't like daddy to be like that!" Arthur decided right then that he would beat the odds and walk again. Today he is a success in his civilian job, a success in the National Guard, and a success as a father and family man. He says that his near loss, his handicap, has given him the necessary determination to know he will always be able to beat the obstacles. His life would not be nearly so full if he had not almost lost it.

This whole concept of acceptance may strike you as a far-fetched ideal to preach, but it is actually achievable if we approach it slowly and patiently. The secret?

GET OFF BY
YOURSELF TO WORK ON YOU

As we learned earlier, these feelings of acceptance and relaxation can be achieved through "creative visualization" or the "quiet room" technique. If we can practice self-respect vividly, within our mind's eye, and practice this skill under minimal pressure, then little by little our real behavior can begin to change. It has been said that if you hold a picture of yourself in your mind's eye long enough, you will become what you think about. In his book, <u>Think and Grow Rich</u>, Napoleon Hill says, **"You are who you think you are."** Elsewhere, it has been said, **"That which you can see and believe, you can achieve."**

If we can remember, in detail, some of our past successes so that we re-experience them, the feeling can carry over into our real actions. If we can really see ourselves performing well, then we should be able to do it.

Consider, for example, how much courage and determination Arthur Gray musters up each and every time he thinks back to his victory over the wheelchair. Review in your mind some of your past successes from your high school or college years or some previous job you had. After a little reflection on those experiences, you might be amazed at the renewed enthusiasm and confidence you display.

No matter what your present condition or feelings are like, you can rest assured that you are that way and feel that way for perfectly legitimate reasons. It's natural for you to be what you are and to feel as you do right now. However, once you embrace the idea that you can be successful, you will find yourself forming small mental images, getting new hunches and ideas, walking around with new and appropriate feelings, and putting ideas together in different and exciting ways. You'll feel more hopeful and enthusiastic, gradually picking up excitement and energy and, little by little, turning the vision into reality.

This does not mean you should expect a life free of problems and difficulties. They will come. As we said earlier, it is necessary to have problems and some hardships to really appreciate and enjoy the good times and rewards. There are many people, speakers and motivators who state such things as, "There are no such things as problems, only challenges!" That sounds really great, but who are we kidding? Trying to play semantics or word games is silly. We have problems, difficulties, challenges, or whatever label you choose to put on them. The real "challenge" is trying to figure out how to handle them.

We cannot force ourselves to believe life is going to be perfect or that we're going to have absolute success. Most of us cannot honestly say that we are sure we're going to make it. If we do, it may ring false, and when it rings false, it can mean that our real basic feeling is fear and doubt. We begin to build self-assurance by taking smaller bites — gradual doses of faith and optimism when they are meaningful and true.

A lady named Joan followed this principle. Joan was certain her business superiors didn't like her. She complained to the personnel director. "Why don't you think they like you?" the director asked her. "It's just their attitude toward me. They gave me a raise a while back, but they tried to make me feel awfully indebted for it." "How?" asked the personnel director. "Oh, just the look on their faces." The personnel director looked at her directly. "Joan, is it just possible that you could be wrong? I'm sure I overheard both of your bosses say the other day that you well deserved a raise. Would you just toy with the idea that you could be wrong? I could easily be wrong myself, but just watch them. I think they actually do like you."

Joan started making herself try to communicate with her bosses in an expectant rather than a defensive attitude. She also experimented with the application of this principle to other areas. "It really is possible," she'd say, "that I got promoted on my own merits. It is possible after all." Even saying these words cheered her up. "Maybe more people think I'm okay than I thought before." Using this same optimistic frame of mind, she applied it to many other areas. Soon her attitude of "it is possible" became generalized. Life was full of possibilities for her.

When he was dying, the famous Russian scientist Pavlov was asked what it took to be successful. Almost with his last breath, he sighed out with conviction, "Passion and gradualness!"

His words are something to remember and apply. All of us may feel bad or experience negative thoughts from time to time. It is a normal human condition brought on by countless experiences and developed unconsciously in your "computer." It's just that old "comfort zone" restricting us. By learning how your mind and emotions interact with experience, you can begin reshaping certain aspects of your life. **Overcoming and outgrowing unhappiness is one of the greatest of all human achievements.** It is possible to accomplish and you can do it.

8

THE SUCCESSFUL PERSONALITY

YOU ARE THE MASTER

In his million-plus seller book, <u>The Greatest Salesman in the World</u>, Og Mandino says, **"I will live this day as if it is my last."** His point is that we should strive to make this the best day of our lives. He continues, "I will live this day as if it is my last. And if it is not, I shall fall to my knees and give thanks." He drills away at the point that we should not waste a second worrying about yesterday nor a second of concern about what might go wrong tomorrow. All you really have is now —today! Make it count.

By now you are aware that your life, **happiness, and success are completely your responsibility.** No one is going to spend his or her whole life doing your feeling for you or urging you to do well. You are on your own. You are the master of your own fate. You can draw support from others. You can draw support based on your faith. But in the end, **it is up to you to determine what kind of life you will have.**

Here is an example of a young man who relied on someone else for his happiness and success rather than on himself. Bill was a sales manager in his father's small, but profitable furniture operation. Bill had always been able to depend on "good old dad" who had put him through school. When he couldn't find employment elsewhere, his dad hired him as a salesman and he did well — when he worked. The problem was he liked golf and playing with his children and pursued fun just a little too much. His wife noticed this element in his character and asked him if he were running scared for some reason. He denied it with a sudden, startling, anger and resentment that even surprised him a bit. About two weeks after his wife confronted him, Bill's father suffered a sudden stroke and was disabled permanently. The employees who respected his father stayed on for a while to work with Bill. Through long association, however, they knew he wouldn't be much of a manager. The salespeople could not rely on Bill and they left in a very short time. It became hard for Bill to hire new people. He had never learned to live on his own or to develop his own talents and abilities. The business went down hill and was sold eighteen months after his father's stroke. Bill was trying to rely on others for his own success and happiness. It cost him a great deal.

CHARACTERISTICS
OF THE SUCCESSFUL PERSON

Let's look at the successful and happy personality. Here is a partial list of the factors that make up the success-prone individual.

1. Self -Acceptance:

You should realize that by now, self-acceptance is the most important prerequisite you have for happiness and success. A high degree of self-acceptance is based on a genuine and accurate knowledge of yourself and how you developed mentally, emotionally and socially. It implies a wide and informed knowledge of your own humanity and the humanity you share with every man, woman and child. This ability is one of the most important human abilities one can develop. A song by Whitney Houston, "The Greatest Love of All," makes this point strongly when she says, **"Learning to love yourself is the greatest love of all".**

Accepting the truth about yourself, however, is not always easy, but as long as you try to hide from yourself, you will most likely be uneasy, unable to fit in comfortably, unable to have honest relationships with others, and prone to temperamental defensive outbursts.

It has been the observation of every great philosophy, religion and school of psychology that man is at the same time the marvel and the disgrace of the universe. This is true of mankind in general and individually. There are some truths about us that we are proud of while other personal truths may disgust us.

We may find that despite our brilliance, quick mind, and charming personalities, what we are really doing is trying to win the approval of others. For example, when Sally Field accepted her second Academy Award, the highest honor for an actor, she said, "You do like me, you really do like me."

We may find that hidden in our every action and feeling is a constant striving for admiration and praise. We may find that the self-image from which we function is one of a scared and lonely individual attempting to conquer these fears. It may be hard to admit all truths about ourselves, but it is a first step toward self-acceptance. Only then can we learn to live for different reasons and learn to seek values and rewards that build success.

Most great men and women, at one time or another, have had to recognize the truth about themselves and then set about with a determination to be a better person. They clearly saw not only the truth that hurts, but also the truth that turns people into successes. This clear vision of themselves and the acceptance of the person they saw as valuable made the difference.

As we stated earlier, sometimes the truth hurts. Sometimes we have people in classes who discover personal "truths" that are hard to take, even in a positive environment. Usually their built in defense mechanism causes them to lash out at us or to complain about the course. Fortunately, they are usually able to work their way through it and complete the program by finding a very valuable person underneath all the flaws.

We tell participants, "If you walk out the door at the end of the week a better salesperson, a better manager, a better leader, or a better whatever, it will be because you walk out the door as a better person."

Try to find out what you really think you're worth. Accept both the good and the bad. No matter what your self-image may be, if you accept that individual, he will come alive and go to work for you. Remember, **all human beings are valuable, and every basic personality has excellent qualities.** Accept the truth that hurts with honesty; don't lie to yourself. Accept the truth of your value with gratitude, enthusiasm and determination.

2. Enthusiasm:

A second important factor is enthusiasm. The word enthusiasm originated in ancient Greek from the words "en theos." Translated literally, these words mean "in God" or "in the Spirit." It might best be described as vitality and eagerness, an intensity of feeling, a fervor. **True enthusiasm is not just a sudden burst of emotional energy but rather a form of deep peace and strong emotional current.** From an individual point of view, it can be acquired and its achievement is born of an open and honest searching and appreciation for life. Enthusiasm must be real and constant. In terms of leadership, **a leader must have enough enthusiasm for himself or herself and enough to allow others to take out a loan or to borrow some.**

People in many of our seminars speak about enthusiasm. From thousands of their talks, we've learned a tremendous amount about true enthusiasm and the broad spectrum that is covered by that one word. Hundreds have talked about coaching or working with kids, teaching handicapped people, working with the Special Olympics, their kids' home runs, etc. Others may tell of the birth of their child, a special relationship with a friend, parent, grandparent or other relative. Some talk about a religious experience, some a personal accomplishment. Still others tell of a tragic occurrence or a devastating illness of a family member. It is sometimes difficult to determine why they would focus on an unpleasant event when the assigned topic is enthusiasm. Inevitably, their conclusion demonstrates the strength, courage, determination, and enthusiasm for life that was gained from the experience. One thing we've learned for certain is that enthusiasm is not limited to pom-poms and football games, and it definitely goes deeper than backslapping and one liners!

Enthusiasm can grease life's runways. It's worth developing the habit of being enthusiastic. Some people seem to have been born with enthusiasm. But don't kid yourself. They choose to be that way. They generate enthusiasm in themselves and in others.

3. **Ability to Relax**:

It includes the ability to take one thing at a time, to live in the present, and to clear your mind before taking on other concerns. It helps you to focus your attention more effectively. It implies confidence, humor and presence of mind. It includes a worthwhile self-image. The "quiet room" technique discussed earlier can help build calmness and aid the process of relaxation. Used properly, we can even relax from physical and emotional pain.

Difficult as it may seem, to relax from pain is frequently sound practice. Psychologists studying the nature of physical and mental pain have found out that suffering, by its nature, is usually short and intense. Prolonged or chronic pain is often stress related and, consequently, inhibits relaxation. These researchers have found that the worst aspect of emotional and bodily pain can be the powerful distress resistance that people set up inside themselves to resist the pain itself. It is the individual's own inner attitude of rejection that can make the most unbearable agony.

In recent years, doctors have found much success in using bio-feedback in treating some illnesses such as migraine headaches. This process teaches the patients how to mentally refocus their attention away from the pain and toward some enjoyable pastime.

Consider another example. One of the most massive human sufferings is child birth. Typically, women in labor furrow their faces and do everything they can to fight the spasms and contractions. Some doctors, consequently, decided to go the other direction. Rather than fight nature and the natural reactions and feelings taking place, why not try to surrender to the process, flow along with the feelings, and cooperate with the pain. The results? Nearly painless childbirth! The mother (depending on her ability to go along with, rather than resist, the enactment) frequently has a beautiful human experience. The "Lamaz" method of natural childbirth is a very popular alternative that is chosen by thousands of women each year.

The message here is somewhat similar to one of Christ's sayings, **"Do not resist evil, but overcome evil with good"**. A psychologist might say "Don't resist painful things, but rather experience them fully and overcome them by suffering the situation with surrender and cooperation." Often our inability to relax is our inability to cope with certain feelings and ideas that stir in us as soon as we slow down, thus we stay busy doing something constantly.

One form of mental concentration and meditation is to sit down and completely surrender to those feelings which do not allow us to relax. If we do, we may find ideas, images and feelings racing around inside at terrific speed. By allowing them to come out, the feelings exhaust themselves and deep peace may follow.

Another tried and proven method to aid relaxation is exercise. Researchers studying stress have concluded that **three specific factors can strongly contribute to stress reduction—relaxation, exercise, and a proper diet.** The exercise not only strengthens your whole body, but it also allows you to work out, sweat out, or "milk" your body of toxins and waste that can cause your body to actually store up stress. Muscles can get tight, digestion can become poor, and your health can rapidly go to pot! Exercise is certainly a constructive method of coping with stress. People who learn to relax have a longer, more successful and enjoyable life.

4. Patience:

Someone once said that **the very definition of maturity is the ability to wait**. Patience implies tolerance of self, of others, and the conditions around you. It implies the ability to listen. True patience implies the ability for daily persistent effort. If your self-concept includes a patient self, it is easier for you to attain maturity.

5. Ability to Forgive:

True forgiving has nothing to do with the person you forgive. He or she doesn't owe you anything because you forgive him. It doesn't make you morally superior to him. Forgiveness is something you do in order to remain peaceful and happy inside.

6. Empathy or Understanding:

A person who is truly understanding and empathetic has the ability to see things as others see them, feel things as others feel them, and treat others the way he or she wants to be treated. Sound familiar? For two thousand years we've heard: **"Do unto others, as you would have them do unto you."**

Understanding implies insight, awareness, and a respect for differences. It further implies the ability to communicate. It is expressed beautifully in the maxim, "Don't disagree with anyone until you can repeat back to the person what he is trying to say to you—to his satisfaction." Understanding implies the ability to listen attentively and accurately. It leads to friendship and eliminates prejudice. If you are able to truly see yourself as an understanding person, you have developed a valuable characteristic of success.

7. Courage:

If you make decisions and actually do things, you are going to be wrong sometimes. **It takes courage to be wrong and risk failure.** Courage is the ability to make a decision regardless of how things may come out. It is the ability to face the truth, admit mistakes, take the offensive, and bet on yourself. It means doing what you know is right. It means definiteness of spirit, standing alone, accepting responsibility, and being willing to get hurt and make mistakes. It is, moreover, the ability to think well of yourself and others no matter what they think of you.

8. Generosity:

Robert Woodruff, the Coca-Cola Company magnate that built that company into the single most recognizable symbol on earth, made a statement that applies here. "There is no limit to what a man can do or where he can go if he doesn't mind who gets the credit." Mr. Woodruff made another statement about generosity, too. During his lifetime he personally gave away over three hundred million dollars!

Whether by giving credit to others, sharing wealth with others, serving others or whatever — **successful people contribute. They are givers, not takers.**

Spend some time thinking about the characteristics we have discussed. Also, don't forget about characteristics we've discussed earlier such as determination and persistence. You might be wise to go back and review this discussion in Chapter Two. More importantly, consider the extent to which each applies to you. Then prepare to make success a habit and a journey.

9

SUCCESS IS A HABIT AND A JOURNEY

DEVELOPING A SUCCESS HABIT

You have learned that self-confidence is built on a series of small successes and that as these successes continue, they result in a more positive self-image and a more healthy ego. Self-confidence and a positive self-image are important contributors to acquiring a success habit.

One of the most significant things that will take place as you develop a success habit is that you will begin to notice a change. At first you may realize that you are noticing things you hadn't seen before — beauty, colors, nature, animals, etc. You may then realize that you are enjoying these things and are more open to new ideas. What you are really experiencing is self-realization, or more specifically, self-acceptance. *(You are now beginning to feel the real secret of success.)* This is probably one of the most rewarding periods of adjustment when you begin to attain the feeling of success. What you have actually done is given up some bad habits or discarded a good share of your negative thinking. This whole area of attitude development could further be illustrated by the analogy of the individual who has given up smoking. The individual who no longer smokes becomes more aware of tastes and smells that have previously been dulled by his smoking habit.

Consider another example of a changing or developing attitude. **An attitude can be changed in a split second**. During one of our seminars Roy Espiritu came in the door on the first morning looking like death warmed over. Roy had participated in a previous class, and, although he really enjoyed it, he didn't want to be there again. He had made up his mind that the week was going to be a waste since he had already had the course. We knew this wasn't his usual manner. He was allowing himself to be totally negative. The question was posed to the group, "How long does it take to change your attitude?" After a few moments of silence, Roy almost shouted, "It only takes one second!" In that one second Roy did something else. He changed his own attitude. Suddenly, the old Roy came alive and started to enjoy himself and set the pace for the rest of the group!

The change that you begin to see and feel in yourself can best be described as an awareness, or better still, an awakening of your sensitivities. This awakening and, consequently, the success habit are developed and cultivated through conscious effort. They are the end result of your positive planning and attainment of your goals.

THE ROLE OF YOUR SUPPORT GROUP

Many people have difficulty recognizing their own progress in the area of self development until they take a serious look at themselves. As we stated earlier, most of us are inclined to look at the other person and think he or she is smarter, more attractive, stronger, sexier...you name it. They've got it all. The problem is that we have trouble overlooking our flaws and focusing on our good points and our improvement as we develop.

Sometimes we need help from a supportive spouse or friend to force us to recognize this growth. In the case of one individual it was necessary for his wife to point out some of the improvements he had made. Often personal development may be so gradual that it is taken for granted. In the case of this person, he became aware that he liked people more. In addition, he had gradually become more involved in his community and was promoted in his job. When he probed deep into his living patterns, he realized he was smoking less and the pains in his stomach were gone. The changes that were pointed out to him were the beginning of self-realization.

This shows the importance of team work in the family unit for recognizing development and how gradual and natural it can be. Be sure you don't overlook the true value of your support group. Also, recognize that this man's spouse pointed out his improvements instead of focusing on his faults. We don't need our support group to butcher us — just support us. You can't force change on others. They have to decide they want the change.

BE PATIENT WITH YOURSELF

Many people fail to recognize that **everyone does not grow or learn at the same rate.** The important fact is that with application of the principles of positive growth, we will all grow and we will continue to grow at our own rate.

Terry belonged to an unusually enthusiastic group that we instructed. He regarded the progress of his classmates as superior and considered himself to be very reserved. It was a struggle to keep him enthused and attending class because he always seemed to feel that he was behind. With hesitating and stumbling steps, he plodded his way through the course. About two years later he appeared in our office a noticeably different person. He had finally decided to give sales a try. He said that after graduation he realized that while he wasn't just like his classmates, his attitude had improved and that he also liked his job better. He had started to feel better about himself, and this made his outlook for the future brighter and more hopeful.

What he had recognized in himself was that he grew differently and at a different rate than his classmates.

When given proper direction and the right encouragement, a person can develop far beyond his or her wildest expectations. As attainments become noticeable to the individual, feelings of self-confidence, self-esteem, or self-respect are developed.

THE WHAT, HOW AND
WHY OF SELF-CONFIDENCE

Self-confidence seems to be the most sought after quality among all professional fields. Just what is self-confidence? How do we know when we have self-confidence? Why do you need it?

Webster defines it as a "belief in one's own ability, power or judgment." The stronger this belief, the greater the commitment one has to it and the stronger his or her confidence is. There isn't much room in this definition for the possibility of doubt, fear, indecision or the greatest crippler of mankind, failure. **The confident person doesn't really worry about these things. He or she simply dives in with determination and an attitude of complete expectancy of success.** Any apprehension can be used as fuel for success. Self confidence is also connected with great feats of courage such as the landing of astronauts on the moon. When asked if they had any fears regarding the moon landing, the answer was, "No, we were confident of our training and preparation and felt ready for any eventuality." They indicated they had no fears, but were anxious to be on their way to one of man's greatest adventures in space.

How do we know when we have self-confidence? One basic answer is when you have the ability to face tough situations and you know that you have the ability to handle them.

Sometimes our confidence can get a tremendous boost from an unlikely source — a compliment from a person we respect, admiration from a child, reflecting on how we handled an emergency situation, or perhaps how we lived through a tragedy. Mike Christensen, for example, is a friend from Idaho. Several years ago

Mike was involved in an accident. A high voltage power line hit him across the face. After thirteen days in a coma and eighteen operations over the next four years, Mike said he realized that nothing he could ever face would be tougher than what he had already been through. He said, "I'm still the same person. I like myself, and if the scar on my face bothers others, that's OK. I'm alive! God let me live through this thing for a reason. He gave me another chance and I am going to make the best of it!" Certainly, our confidence grows when we have a faith that is this strong!

Why do we need self-confidence? Psychologists have long recognized the human need we have for approval, acceptance, respect and love. These contribute to a feeling of adequacy and are paramount in the enhancement of self-confidence. People tend to look up to the confident individuals and have trust in them. For example, our elected officials are simply an extension of our confidence in them. We need confidence in ourselves to communicate our best to our co-workers, our customers, our employers and our loved ones. Confidence, in this case, reinforces the feeling that you are doing the right thing at the right time.

Success is a combination of many things. Just as self-confidence plays an important role in achieving success, so does the right attitude. **Negative people are a pain.** Just think for a minute (or even an hour.) Try to think of one single negative person you enjoy being around. Bet you can't do it. The positive, enthusiastic individuals are the ones we enjoy. Positive people seem to like everyone and radiate good feeling and love for their fellow man. One good friend, an insurance professional, says that the reason for his success in the insurance business is that he sincerely loves his clients. People buy from him because he really cares about them and they can sense it. He is one of the most optimistic and well liked people in his profession. He is an extremely generous, giving person. He is optimistic in his faith. He enjoys people and enjoys helping them. At the same time, he is helping himself by earning a more than substantial living and winning national honors from his company.

The opposite side of the coin is the extreme pessimist or the negative person. He or she is incapable of loving his fellow man because he first of all doesn't love himself. After all, we are told, "Love your neighbor as you love yourself." The negative person is likely to be suspicious and uncooperative with his fellow workers and is probably known as the company complainer. This individual is apathetic in his relationship with others. Continuation of his prophecy of doom is poison to the atmosphere of any company. If, for an instant, you recognize yourself anywhere in this last paragraph, you may have just gained insight into a reason for any inconsistency in your achievement of success.

LAUGH AT YOURSELF

Upon entering the Army, the young military novice is subjected to many lectures concerning what his conduct will be as a representative of the United States Armed Forces. One particular lecture was given by a Battalion Chaplin. As his major point he stated, "If you want to get along in the Army, ladies and gentlemen, you must maintain your sense of humor." He was right and he was right for civilian life as well. Too many people take themselves too seriously and have great difficulty seeing the humor in life because of their total preoccupation with self. Whether on the tennis court, golf course, or wherever — lighten up and maintain the ability to laugh at yourself. Accept the fact that you simply aren't perfect. **Take your responsibilities seriously, but not yourself**. The ability to laugh at yourself will see you through many uncomfortable situations. The key is to involve yourself outside of your present realm of knowledge and expand your area of concern. Try showing concern for someone else. It is impossible to worry about yourself and someone else simultaneously.

With a good sense of humor and real concern or empathy for others, it is easier to develop a good sense of direction. In the establishment of a worthwhile life, it is important to know where you are going. It is not necessary to be totally planned, but a general description of the direction in which you are heading is vitally important. Somehow, with a firm direction in mind and some of the basic steps before you, the rest will fall into place as you take your journey in forming the habit of success.

10

BECOMING GOALS ORIENTED

Success has been described as a journey and not a destination. But without a destination, end result, or goal to be achieved, there is no reason to start on any journey. If we are to become successful, we must first establish goals that are meaningful and worthy of our efforts. If we do this, we can have enjoyment along the way as we reach the desired goals. We must think in terms of end results, and then follow a plan. Your goals must become the road maps you live by. When you take an automobile trip across the country, you follow maps in choosing a route, and you plan the trip with specific destinations. Your goals should be dealt with in the same manner.

DEFINING SUCCESS

So what exactly is success? We like to define success as:

The accomplishment, or progress toward accomplishment of your goals in life, whatever they may be — without interfering

with the rights of others.

Notice, this definition allows for the journey and does not limit the focus only to the end result.

To put the word success properly into perspective, perhaps we should examine the opposite end of the spectrum — failure. What exactly is failure?

First of all, failure to accomplish a specific goal, task, or objective is not a tremendously big deal. This is going to happen to all of us many times as we go through life, perhaps even as we go through this day, this week, or this month!

Certainly, in simple form, failure could be defined as "the inability to accomplish your goals."

This sounds like a simple case of opposites, right? Now let's add a twist. Rather than just "inability to accomplish goals," let's put it this way: **A true failure is one who will not put out the effort to accomplish his or her goals. He is one who gives in to the obstacles and quits trying.**

APPRAISING YOUR PRESENT GOALS

When establishing goals in life, we begin with short term goals on our way to larger ones. Before you can set a goal of any kind, however, **you must first determine what you have to work with and where you are now by appraising your present situation**. As with the trip, you check out the car to determine if it is fit to make the trip. You take into consideration your finances, the time involved, and various pieces of equipment you will need for your journey. Only an idiot starts out without proper planning and preparation.

WEIGH YOUR
STRENGTHS AND WEAKNESSES

Second, as a part of appraising your present situation, you must also **weigh your personal strengths and weaknesses.** In fact, much of this book has been devoted to helping you do exactly that.

Hopefully, as you read this material, it helped you take a long hard look at yourself, considering your attributes that help you as well as your weak points that may be holding you back.

DETERMINE WHAT YOU WANT

Third, you decide on a goal to be achieved and whether or not you are adequately prepared to make the journey. You decide what is to be accomplished when you reach the goal and why you want to reach that particular objective. This "why" gives you the incentive to carry on.

It is, more or less, your purpose — the force that gives you the extra drive and determination to accomplish the objective. Your purpose, however, can be a real bear to define. **You are the only person on earth who can establish your priorities or your purpose in life**. To some people, family is more important. To others a career is paramount. Some combine the two, while still others seem to care about nothing at all.

Recognize this — there are only two ways to demonstrate your priorities:

1. How you spend your time.
2. How you spend your money.

If you really care about someone or something, you'll spend time and/or money to demonstrate that care.

Clearly defining your purpose, the most important thing in your life, will shape every single aspect of your existence. Does this sound serious? We hope so—because it is! Until you really identify your purpose, you'll flounder around trying to figure out what you want. Take the time now to figure it out!

DEVELOPMENT
AND SCHEDULING OF YOUR PLANS

Next, like the trip, you spread out the maps and set a day-by-day plan of progress to be made over a particular period of time. You set the timetable for achievement and then work to stay on schedule. To accomplish this can take great effort and sacrifice. This means giving up many less important things to stay on target.

CONVERT YOUR PLANS INTO ACTION

When the journey begins, you must convert your plans into action and follow through. It is here where many people stumble and fall. The best made plans often crumble because the maps for the journey didn't show the obstacles. Often we also over-estimated our ability to reach a particular destination at a particular time.

Rather than readjust their plans and begin a new course of action, many people give up entirely. Remember what we said about true failure? It is someone who won't put out the effort or who gives in to the obstacles and quits trying. In this situation, it is important to review all the reasons for deciding on a given goal and why it was planned in the first place. It is important to dig in again and re-evaluate the plan and time schedule. Keeping the goal constantly in mind, you then push forward. To begin a journey and not arrive is like running a hundred yard dash and quitting after ninety-nine yards. Why run at all?

Develop a habit of thinking in terms of goals. **The more often you start a journey and fail to finish, the more you develop failure habits** and can soon lack the self confidence in your ability to achieve. It can become easy to quit at the first hint of a problem.

Goal achievement is built upon successful goal achievement. The person without a goal is like a ship without a rudder. He or she aimlessly drifts through life. It is now up to you to set your sights and move in a meaningful direction toward accomplishing your life's ambition.

BECOMING GOALS ORIENTED
(Completing this page can give you a quick start
on becoming more goals oriented.)

1. Determine, as best you can, what you feel is your purpose in life — what you feel is most important to you. You may find it helpful to try to complete the sentence, "Here lies a person who...," as though you were writing your own epitaph.

_____

_____

_____

_____

_____

2. Considering all aspects of your life and your purpose (as listed above), list your priorities here. Be sure to consider such things as: career, family, friends, religion, possessions, fame, wealth, etc.

_____

_____

_____

3. Consider a goal you have accomplished in the past: What was it? _____

_____

_____

   How did this accomplishment make you feel? _____

_____

_____

4. List a goal you want to accomplish: _____

   When will you start? _____

   When will you complete it? _____ _____

   What is your first step? _____

We hope this material has given you some guidance and a stronger sense of direction. If you read it conscientiously, it should have functioned like a mirror. The mirror on your wall, however, only shows the outside. Hopefully, this book helped you to take a pretty close look at the inside. You may find, as many others have, that it will pay great dividends to re-read this material from time to time. After all, you are a dynamic individual, one who is constantly in a state of change. Consequently, this book will say something different to you each time you read it.

Accept yourself. Decide that you like yourself — even LOVE yourself. Do those things that cause you to like yourself even more, and we promise you this: You will
DEVELOP AN ATTITUDE FOR SUCCESS!

Good Luck!